MW01644910

World War ‘D’

The Intersection of Cyber and Biological
Pandemics

Christopher Rence

ISBN: 9798825081908

Dedication

To my parents for always supporting me. There wasn't a parenting book that could have prepared you for my inquisitive nature that you always encouraged.

I have not made it to Mars, but I am still trying.

Acknowledgment

To Irwin L. Jacobs, Charles Porter, Tom Grudnowski, Mark Pautch, Paul Larson, Myke Miller, Joel Ronning, and Debora Kerr for all of their insight and reality checks that have helped me continue to strive forward.

CONTENTS

About the Author

Christopher J. Rence is a C-level leader with more than 25 years of success driving profitable and sustainable business growth. An innovative leader and a global security data protection expert, he has a history of creating long-term value and leading transformation initiatives across global teams for Accenture, FICO, Digital River, and Equus Holdings. He is an expert in GDPR, DPO, CIPPE, CRISC, CISO, MBCP, and global security data and cloud protection for technology and technology-enabled businesses. Known for accelerating meaningful innovation and business growth through visionary and strategic thought leadership, Christopher's high-integrity leadership style unifies and inspires people, ideas, and teams. He is a tenacious problem solver who elevates performance in technology, process, and individuals and thrives on building cultures where out-of-the-box thinking is expected in an environment that embraces transformative change and growth.

Chris is currently the president and CEO of Rimage Corporation and Rence Communication and Compliance. He also serves on several boards as a member.

Preface

You, the reader, whether you are a global leader or pulling your livelihood from a trash dump, do need to know or accept what a cyber pandemic is; you do need to know or accept what a biological pandemic is. You do need to accept that these forces that either evolved from technology, nature, or mankind are influencing and changing your life, and both can end it without any remorse or consequences. Your memory will be short-lived among the ones that survived, a headstone or the bits of data held across the technology wasteland. These two forces will always be in the shadows, and you will be infected and affected at some time in your life. These forces are always changing, so your ability to escape their invasion into your cells or the technology you depend on is futile.

Chapter 1

Introduction

The future is now. We are in a global cyber pandemic that is influencing, changing, and defining our technical, economic, and DNA future not only on Earth but also as we return to the moon and explore Mars. Even if you think you can escape into the Metaverse, you are wrong. The reach and depth of the cyber pandemic will invade your alternative universe, and the technology bridge will have consequences that you will never recover from.

The year 2020 changed the world for good; no one expected a global pandemic when they heard the news of a new breed of virus out of China. Was it designed, did it evolve, and who is its target? Nine billion people and mother nature are doing what she can to correct her mistakes. Governments are racing to develop the perfect deterrent weapon while people are strictly following the SOPs.

The first cases were reported in December of 2019, and by the end of 2020, a hundred million cases and over two and a half million deaths worldwide were reported resulting from the virus. We were all naïve and ignorant at the beginning of the pandemic, and in a few months, the virus shut down global borders and brought the world's leaders to their knees. Curfews were enforced, and schools and workplaces were shut down. A few weeks and, for some, months passed by until businesses couldn't bear any more losses. Schools and businesses started testing out different platforms to go online and remain operational. It took some time, but people adapted to working from home and online classes. Some workplaces became even more efficient as a result and decided to remain online permanently.

Most businesses didn't oversee the level of security in their networks when employees were working from outside the boundaries of office controls. It was challenging to monitor and provide security for each employee spread out through the country. Soon, we started seeing the consequences of this oversight. 2020/2021 was the worst year, not just due to the biological pandemic but also because of the cyber pandemic, as this year saw the highest recorded number of cyber-attacks in history. Here are some statistics for reference.

- Thirty thousand websites were hacked daily.
- Sixty-four percent of companies worldwide faced at least one type of cyber-attack.

- There is a new attack somewhere on the internet every thirty-nine seconds.
- Twenty-four thousand malicious applications are blocked every day.

And the list goes on and on. Compared to 2019, ransomware attacks grew by nearly four hundred percent, that's almost four times the amount since the previous year!

The world changed overnight, and we adapted to it, but so did the hackers and cybercriminals. We are seeing a new breed of Cyber Mercenaries for hire, hackers for hire, ransomware as a service (RAAS), and enterprise-level tools and servers to help manage this new Dark Web of consulting services. This is why we are all players in the new game of WWD, even if we do not know it.

The false security we wrap ourselves in, hoping that the other guy or the tools and services we have invested in, even at the lowest level, will protect us, is fleeting.

The Dark Web is becoming the e-commerce for obtaining off the shelf roadmaps to your systems architecture, the data you hold, the tools and processes needed to access your environments, either physical or logical, and your R&D.

The most challenging subject is your future. The bad actors do not need a chute down to your systems; they do not need to ask you for cryptocurrencies; they can alter your future for their gain. AI and ML can be deployed to influence buyers, like what happened with GameStop, and cause massive damage before the circuit breakers can trip. The next great idea that one of your staff is playing with just got picked up through a Phishing campaign and distributed to your competitors or just given away for free.

How about ransomware at the molecular level? Say you or someone you know is going in for a medical procedure, and the bad actors already know because of the PII records at hospitals. Employers and insurance companies around the world have had their databases accessed frequently. You may receive a text saying give me “x,” or something might go wrong; the prescriptions may be altered, the power might go out, the applications that drive the MRI/CT scans can be altered to point out or emit information that will change your life forever.

Every tool and operating system across all platforms is vulnerable; do not fool yourself. From Microsoft to every flavor of Linux, Kylin, Mac OS, every phone operating system is at risk. So, stop and think. The average combustion engine car has twenty to fifty processors performing all tasks from performance to defensive processes like airbags and seatbelt functions. The new electric cars have, on average, a hundred to two hundred processors performing all the functions. The next big hack will be on your car. I wonder what kind of attack the hackers from the underbelly of the web will orchestrate by taking control of our cars.

IOT is everywhere; your home, your car, and the planes you are traveling in. The warheads, missiles, and nuclear devices all have processors that can be hacked with enough time and due diligence.

This is the new world, data is the center of everything, and no one, no government, country, or system, is exempt unless your data is based on an offline non-alterable, non-digital medium.

Since the 2000s, technology has been advancing and growing exponentially, so fast that the rules regulating technology are based on antiquated laws and policies. Some of these laws haven't been changed in the past thirty years, which is when they were first enforced. Technology has gone so far that, based on algorithms and artificial intelligence, hackers are able to produce three hundred thousand new pieces of malware daily. You may think that just because you haven't encountered a blue screen or a Trojan virus, your computers and data are safe, but you would be wrong to make any such assumptions. There are untraceable viruses and file extensions that disguise themselves as necessary files on your computers. These files keep an eye on your activities and data while you're under the false pretense that some anti-virus software protects your intellectual property.

When you think of the Corona Virus, think about the data network that drives your body. With the network under attack, you've seen how quickly nations and various institutions have scrambled to create a vaccine. When the virus mutated into several variants, it drove even more investment and resources into helping build more defense against the new variant(s).

Now, consider the world's vast digital data network and enter the Cyber Pandemic, where there are new viruses every day, targeted and independent bits of malware, socially engineered to target data belonging to individuals, companies, and even governments. These hackers plant ransomware in your devices that shadows you and learns from your routines and habits to manufacture viruses that extract vital personal data like credit card information, personal photos, and confidential files. They then use this data to extort you, steal from you, influence you and even watch you. Nothing about your identity remains personal anymore. These hackers are primarily financially motivated; about eighty-six percent of all data breaches globally are financially motivated. This number has increased by fifteen percent during the pandemic compared to the previous year.

Earlier, hackers were more motivated by grudges or

revenge, but ever since the pandemic took over the world, there has been a sharp increase in the number of hackers and cybercriminals alongside the frequency and number of cyber-attacks. Many tech companies and software houses shut down in conjunction with a record number of layoffs in the industry. This led a lot of coders and tech experts toward desperation, and they resorted to using their skillset to financially exploit the technologically illiterate and vulnerable individuals and institutions.

Here's another set of data points that hit close to home; not only is the cyber pandemic taking advantage of the fast pace changes due to the Covid-19 pandemic, but they are also targeting the infrastructure that supports our daily lives. Power grids, water treatment plants, hospitals, and all levels of regional and global government organizations are under threat. As the governments try to combat both the biological and cyber pandemics, the rules get bent, not broken, but the privacy you think you have is being overridden. In the background, they all know what you are looking at, who you are texting with, and the topics you are searching for.

So the days of unconditional trust no longer exist; your digital and biological signature is a part of all of the databases being scanned, sorted, and profiled. It is no longer about race, creed, or color but about who, what, and where you were – online, in a restaurant, with whom, and why. So, think about the reality of everything. You are sending out a sonar ping 24x7 with your phone, internet, car, parking meters, traffic cameras, and the like. Even if you are off the grid, the satellites racing around the globe do see everything.

An attempted cyber-attack against a water treatment plant in Florida highlights endemic failures in the cybersecurity of the US water sector. On 5th February, an unidentified attacker accessed the systems at a US water treatment plant in Oldsmar, Florida, and briefly altered the chemical levels in the drinking water.

Even in Europe, infrastructure faced cyber-attacks. The European Network of Transmission System Operators for Electricity or the ENTSO-E fell victim to a cyberattack that adversely affected its office network. The ENTSO-E represents forty-two electricity Transmission System Operators across Europe, which weren't affected by this attack, but a stronger attack could cause a blackout across all of Europe.

Hackers have also been attacking hospitals and their databases a lot recently. The FBI and Cybersecurity and Infrastructure Security Agency said that they have credible information of an increased and imminent cybercrime threat to US hospitals and healthcare providers. This is especially concerning because of how important it is for the medical facilities to stay functioning at this time during a pandemic.

On average, in 2019, it cost companies nearly four million dollars to fix and recover from a data breach, whereas in the US, this number was closer to eight million dollars. Some companies have even spent up to two billion US dollars to recover from a data breach attack on their databases.

In 2016, various large corporations like Uber and Friend finder were victims of massive data breaches, where the user profiles of nearly five hundred million individuals were exposed for anyone to take advantage of. Uber ended up paying the hacker to remove the information from the web and additionally had to pay hundreds of millions in court settlements. Every second, seventy-five records go missing due to cyber-attacks, and in 2018 alone, over half a billion records were stolen from victims around the world.

These kinds of data breaches often occur where the hacker is paid to expose and upload the personal data and details of millions of users to the dark web. This gives hackers enough partial data to discover the IP and Mac addresses of your various devices. They can pin in on your exact location and know which devices you may be logged in from, your laptop, cell phone, gaming console, appliances, etc. Some can even manipulate the actions of your devices. When your data is compromised, others' data on your devices are also at risk, like e-mail addresses and phone numbers.

These hackers have a stronger profile of you and your family than your government or three-letter agencies do. They can access your phone using social engineer techniques to extract data from you, your colleagues, extended family, and even your children. When you are working from home or even remotely from a coffee shop, you are under the virtual and watchful eyes of these cybercriminals who are just waiting for you to let your guard down so they can pounce at the first opportunity you present.

Over ninety percent of all malware is spread through the medium of electronic mail or, in short, e-mail. When you log on to the internet and answer surveys that pop into your inbox all willy-nilly without verification, you are exposing yourself to a potential ransomware attack that may lead to a severe data breach. Similarly, when you leave default passwords on your devices, or when you bypass passwords on your phone, or even answer a few general questions from a mystery caller, you are exposing yourself and your data to a potential breach.

So, what then is the meaning of *'World War D'*? It all lies in the D, D for DATA. When you think of the cyber pandemic and the ongoing war on data, think of what is dear to you. Your money? Your job? Your credit scores? Your identity? Your family? They can take all of that from you; they know where you live, where your parents live, where your kids go to school, your social security number, your bank details, and where you work. Heck, they probably know what you had for lunch yesterday. These hackers are well versed in navigating through the dark web; they have mercenaries and kidnappers on speed dial. They will not hesitate to harm you or your loved ones if you resist their demands or try to negotiate with them.

During the coronavirus pandemic, we learned to wear a mask, use hand sanitizers, stand six feet apart, and self-isolate, if necessary. These measures and practices are now so standard that they've been normalized, and following SOPs is nothing short of second nature for us. However, in the initial stages of the pandemic, there was a spread of misinformation. There was a large portion of people who rejected the idea of a pandemic at all. This didn't change the death toll, and when people experienced the symptoms firsthand or lost loved ones to the virus, they had no choice but to accept the pandemic's presence and severity.

Similarly, the cyber pandemic is no joke. Some people may write all of this off as some conspiracy theory until they're victims of these attacks themselves. Like SOPs for the biological pandemic, there need to be standard practices to ward off the cyber pandemic as well. We're all living in our bubbles in terms of our digital presence. Companies, government institutions, schools, and hospitals are in bubbles of their own. We need to strengthen our bubbles to be impenetrable by external forces.

How you may ask, might one strengthen their bubble? It is quite simple: adding multiple layers of defense to our digital presence. This book will go through, in detail, what you can do, and what preventative measures you can take to protect your data and yourself.

A good anti-virus can serve as a vaccine, routers and firewalls can serve the purpose of hand washing, role-based authentication and user policies are like social distancing, and similarly, a strong password is your mask against malware infection. In the following chapter, we'll go more in-depth, drawing a parallel between the Corona Virus Pandemic and the Cyber Pandemic, analyzing the similarities and how we can effectively combat the adverse effects of the latter.

Some technical terms you need to know about and understand before moving any further are phishing, vishing, social engineering, split tunneling, malware, and ransomware.

Phishing is, perhaps, the most common variety of cyber-attack. The target or victim is contacted via e-mail, instant messaging, text message, or a phone call by someone posing as a legitimate entity trying to get sensitive information out of them like passwords, bank details, credit card details, etc. These calls could be from someone pretending to be from your bank trying to confirm information. The next thing you know, your bank accounts are empty, and the phone number that contacted you has been disconnected. When dealing with such a situation, carefully check the number or e-mail address trying to communicate with you and run it through a search engine to see if you can find that it links to the organization they're claiming they're from. Only after you're a hundred percent sure should you proceed to convey sensitive information over e-mail, text, or phone call.

In most cases, nobody will ask for sensitive personal information over the phone or text anyway. Hackers and scammers will try to lure you in by offering something too good to be true, and that's probably because it is. The scammer may also try to employ urgency to try and get you to blurt out information in a panic. So, be sure you don't give in to such schemes. Also, be very wary of the links you're clicking on. A website may not be all that it seems to be. Carefully read the URL link for spelling errors or discrepancies before clicking it so that you don't end up downloading a virus onto your device. E-mail attachments may also contain harmful malware, so make sure you only download attachments from trusted and verified sources; be cautious of unusual senders and addresses. Turn on spam filters in your e-mail provider's settings because these e-mails are often flagged and will automatically go to the spam folder reducing your likelihood of clicking on any suspicious links or downloading any harmful files. You may also consider installing some kind of extension to your browser that prevents you from accessing harmful sites previously flagged by other users. Some variation of this extension is available for most mainstream web browsers. The goal behind ninety-five percent of phishing e-mails is to use ransomware to extort your company.

Vishing is essentially the same as phishing, but vishers use an internet telephone service or VoIP exclusively to conduct their scams. The concept is the same; they will use unethical and immoral tactics to get sensitive information out of you. By hacking specific VoIP protocols, they are able to spoof legitimate phone numbers; therefore, it becomes quite tricky to suss out vishers. Vishers also harm the reputation of the companies they are spoofing as the call can't be traced back to them. All you can do is not panic and report the phone number if you ever receive such a call. The goal behind a hundred percent of vishing is stealing your identity and quick cash and recurring revenue for the cybercriminals.

Social Engineering is a pretty broad term that encompasses multiple kinds of malicious activities. It is based on human interactions and involves exploiting victims by gaining their trust. These attacks occur in multiple steps; first, the attackers identify a vulnerable subject. Then, they try to gain that person's trust through frequent interactions, eventually coercing them to reveal sensitive information like credit card details and passwords. This is especially difficult to distinguish because it relies on human error instead of a few lines of code.

It's essentially psychological manipulation, and a hacker will try to test and exploit your trust. Trust nobody on the internet! Again, it is vital to be cautious when interacting with others on the internet. Even if you know and trust the person, verify every time and look out for any red flags or irregularities.

Split tunneling enables you to split the flow of your internet traffic using a VPN. It allows you to route some of your traffic through an encrypted VPN tunnel while the rest of your traffic directly accesses the internet. Corporations use VPN split-tunneling to take some load off their corporate networks and divert it through other routes. Using split tunneling has its benefits and downsides as well. It reduces traffic on corporate networks and reduces latency; hence increasing speed and using a VPN also grants an additional layer of privacy to the end-users. Often, larger companies with a higher number of employees on the network will choose to turn on split tunneling while setting up their virtual private network for reduced traffic, increased performance, as well as more privacy. Many businesses suffer from bandwidth constraints, and for tech companies or companies relying on networking, this can cause huge losses if they're offline for even a few minutes.

Split tunneling has become useful for corporations during the pandemic in this era of remote working. It enables employees to access their company's e-mails, corporates files, applications, etc., directly from the server through a VPN with no latency as if they were sitting in the office at their work computer. Still, in reality, they're sitting comfortably at home. However, to use this VPN to access other resources directly from the internet would be quite foolish because this VPN first directs the user to the company's network and then the internet, which can cause latency and slow down the speed of the network. Situations like this are where split tunneling comes in and enables users to access other resources outside the company network by directly connecting them to the internet while, at the same time, allowing them to access the company resources directly from the corporate server through a VPN. Split tunneling has made working from home a breeze for those corporations who have their own VPNs. It even allows much faster communication if users are present on the company network simultaneously.

However, as many benefits as split tunneling provides, it opens up just as many gateways in the private network's security. IT professionals at large companies enforce defensive technologies all over the corporation and secure endpoints that prevent users from accessing certain files or performing tasks that are above their pay grade, be it intentional or accidental. This works best within the confines of the organization's premises, where all users on the network can be monitored and kept in check.

Although, when split tunneling is enabled and users are present in different locations over the map and accessing the company network and the worldwide web at the same time, they can't be monitored to the same effect exposing the corporate network to other public networks as well as the world wide web. If the user accessing the corporate network remotely does not have a secure connection, it poses a significant threat to the corporate network and systems. Suppose a hacker can get into the home network of a company employee who has access to the corporate VPN. In that case, the hacker can also potentially penetrate the company's network, putting it at significant risk. Hackers may do this to access some key files or communications between company employees to extort the company for a huge payout.

When enabling split tunneling, it is imperative to consider these implications and employ relevant security measures and protocols to prevent access by unauthorized individuals to the company network. IT should engage DNS, intrusion detection and prevention systems, as well as data loss prevention systems to prevent unauthorized access to their networks. Even so, these measures are only red tape for hackers, and they will eventually get through because it is impossible to track the usage of so many devices remotely. The larger the employee base working from home, the greater the risk to the company's networks and systems.

An expensive but essential step in ensuring network safety and security is to issue company devices to each employee working from home to be exclusively used for company-related work and tasks. IT can outfit these devices with monitoring software and direct remote access. They can easily monitor and see what sites are being accessed and disallow access to harmful sites and malicious content in this capacity. IT can also block access to sites that cause unproductivity, like social media and streaming sites. Proxy servers may also be enabled to monitor and limit/throttle traffic on the network.

Split tunneling brings with it tremendous advantages like alleviating the load off the network, reducing latency, increasing speed, and providing privacy to the end-users. Still, at the same time, remote working makes the VPN vulnerable to attack and becomes accessible by unauthorized users. To avoid data getting into the wrong hands during this cyber pandemic, corporations should respond accordingly so that they don't have to pay millions in settlement later in court.

Malware, shorthand for malicious software, is an all-encompassing term that includes different variants of viruses, ransomware, and spyware. Typically, it's just a bunch of code not discernible to the likes of the average user, but this code is crafted specially by hackers to do irreversible damage to your digital presence by getting access to your data or network. Malware is, most commonly, disguised within a link or file and is sent over e-mail or requires the user to click a link on the internet or access a particular page that gives the browser permission to download harmful files and execute them. The first known appearance of a virus was recorded in the 1970s, and it was called the creeper virus. Today, uncountable threats are lurking on the internet, way more advanced and engineered to cause harm to digital users.

The most common denomination of malware is a virus. It attaches its code to the clean code of a file or application on your device and waits for you to execute or click on it. Then, like a biological virus, it spreads like cancer and corrupts files that are vital in the running of certain applications. This causes your system to act unusually; apps crash often, many won't function at all, overall performance becomes sluggish, and often the device may shut down entirely. Viruses are so common, in fact, that most malware prevention softwares are known as anti-virus softwares.

Worms are another very infectious kind of malware, but

instead of infecting other files on the same system, they weave and bob through the network affecting and infecting multiple devices on the network. Worms are very quick and can take over all the devices on the same network if not detected and dealt with quickly. Worms can cause significant harm to corporate networks putting work on hold for days and causing a loss of data and files.

As the name suggests, spyware is designed to hide in the background and watch what users are doing on their devices. They collect data and create gateways accordingly for other kinds of malware like viruses or worms. Spyware is often disguised as legitimate software that you let spy on you by agreeing to terms and conditions you never read.

You've probably heard of Trojans before; much like spyware, they're disguised within legitimate software and create backdoors for other kinds of malware to enter the system and infect. Named after the Greek soldiers, they're just as harmful in this war on data.

Also falling under the umbrella of malware, we have ransomware which is potentially the most dangerous of the bunch. Once it infects your system, it will lock you out of using your device properly and demand that you pay a certain fee or enter credit card details holding your personal files and data hostage. If you fail to make the payment, the hacker may permanently corrupt your files or encrypt your hard drive rendering your device useless. It is very difficult to recover from ransomware accounts without succumbing to the demands of the hacker. Ransomware is also known as scareware as it is designed to scare the user into paying large sums of money.

Ransomware has made some of the world's largest organizations kneel as their data was being held hostage. They hired highly skilled coders and hackers to try and retrieve their data without having to pay. However, cybercriminals are always a step or ten ahead with so many fail-safes built into the software that undoing one infection may spread ten new ones throughout the network. In most cases, companies have had no option but to pay the amount.

In 2017, a Korean web hosting firm, Internet Nayana, was struck by a ransomware attack, and the hackers responsible were able to extract over a million US dollars from the company. Beyond monetary losses, ransomware locks you out of your files for as long as the ransom remains unpaid. This could cost companies several days of revenue.

In 2017, a global outbreak of a ransomware attacks infected hundreds of thousands of computers in over a hundred and fifty countries. Besides the billions of dollars of financial losses, it also took the National Health Services in the United

Kingdom by storm, bringing hundreds of healthcare facilities in the UK to a standstill. This attack caused the cancellation of thousands of operations and relocations of emergency patients that needed intensive care.

Historical incidents like these are reminders to large corporations to implement proactive preventative measures to make sure hackers cannot plant such attacks. A few million dollars spent on security now are better than spending hundreds of millions trying to combat such an attack in the future. It is estimated that in 2019, the aggregate ransoms hackers collected up to nearly twelve billion US dollars. Certainly, you've heard of Reckitt Benckiser, and you probably also know what a large organization it is; well, a ransomware attack cost RB over a hundred and forty million US dollars in 2017.

We are amidst the peak of World War D. We must learn about malware and its spread so that we may do whatever we feel necessary to not fall victim to one of these attacks. Preventative measures are extremely important now since a lot of us are working from home and don't have an IT department at our disposal at all times to help us with our problems.

Proceed with extreme caution as you are the first line of defense against these cybercriminals. Everyone is a target; you, your parents, your children, and your peers. Practice the same health and data hygiene that you practice at work and at home. Learn how to recognize phishing and vishing attempts and the tells of malicious software so you may arm yourself and your loved ones with the necessary weapons to stay safe during this war on data.

Some basics you should already be incorporating include updating your operating system to the latest version, as these include critical security patches that are updated every month to protect your devices from newer variants of malware. Along with operating systems, this also applies to other applications; keep them updated for maximum security. Never use default or assigned passwords on devices like routers or for any online profiles. If you have the option, always change your passwords. Set strong passwords with WPA2 encoding on your wireless routers and update their firmware regularly. Stay away from open, public Wi-Fi connections. If you absolutely need Wi-Fi, piggyback off the personal hotspot from your mobile device. Only access work files and data on work computers and keep personal files and data separate with separate devices, if possible. Only use personal devices for work in emergencies and vice versa. Once a printed document has served its purpose, don't throw it directly in the trash; always shred it first, then toss it away.

When prompted to create a password for any new profile,

make sure to use complex passphrases instead of simple words that are common nouns. Make sure the phrase is at least fourteen characters long with complex symbols and numerals. Avoid reusing passwords for multiple profiles as well because, in case of a breach of one account, multiple accounts will be put at risk. Create a system to remember the various passwords for different accounts, like adding an indication of what account the password belongs to in the passphrase. Use these same guidelines to reset any existing passwords you have that may be too simple or don't include symbols and numbers.

Under no circumstances should you share these passwords with a third party. The point of passwords is to allow access only to the owner of the account. If you think someone else knows your password or has seen you type it in, change it immediately. Avoid using personal details like names, phone numbers, and birth dates in your passwords, and never physically write them down. Try to keep your work and personal passwords entirely different to avoid a cross breach if any one of the accounts is compromised. As a rule, you should reset all your passwords after ninety days or three months.

In the current age of smartphones, one should also be aware of the security oversights present in their devices. Most people don't do much to secure data on their cell phones. It's just as important because a cell phone is very easy to steal or probable to get lost, and if it falls into the wrong hands, it can be hacked easily, and all your accounts logged in on that device will be compromised along with any saved credit or debit cards. Also, all contacts on that phone will be at risk as well because the hacker now has their phone numbers and e-mails.

Again, you are the first line of defense, and doing the most straightforward things like setting a password on your phone can make all the difference. Phones today have way more user authentication options like fingerprint sensors, facial recognition software and sensors, retina sensors, patterns, and simple pin codes. Avoid using four-digit pins; they are much easier to crack. Use more extensive pin codes or full passwords for secondary authentication on smartphones. Security patches are especially important for smartphones, so make sure to keep your mobile devices updated as well. Only use instant messaging apps with end-to-end encryption enabled and install apps from verified sources with proper licenses like the Apple App Store or Google Play Store.

All smartphones have a remote wipe option; make sure to turn that on as well and keep your mobile data on so you can use this option when you get mugged or lose your phone. If there are important files and photos on your device, make frequent backups on the cloud and physical drives as well. Don't use public charging stations or tether your device to another device unless both devices belong to you and you're confident they're virus-free.

All of this may sound like it's coming from some manic, foil-hat wearing conspiracy theorist, but you may go to the internet and cross-check any of this information. You'd be shocked to hear how many people fall victim to cybercrimes and have to pay through the nose to make the problem go away. Hopefully, this book will be a complete guide to dealing with all the digital threats you face today and how you can safeguard yourself during this cyber pandemic.

Chapter 2

Cyber Pandemic vs. Global Pandemic

We understand the basics of the cyber pandemic in comparison to the biological pandemic that is restarting with new variations on a global scale. People remember that a biological pandemic, based on history, can take up to 20 years to contain on an international level. During the past pandemics, we did not have the ability to move around the world in hours like we do today, and it took many weeks and months to travel from one place to another. Reality check, most of the world is still waiting to get a vaccine alongside trying to defend itself from unknown cyber pandemics.

Governments all over the world, and local and multinational companies, are contact-switching to managing policy, keeping their workforce safe, and retaining and attracting the needed workforce to maintain their global supply chain.

Our governments have just recently signed executive orders asking for help; it is now official that the cyber pandemic is real. As with our frontline heroes of the biological pandemic who are putting their lives on the line, and as the biological pandemic rollercoasters across the globe, we have come to realize that we do not have enough of these frontline heroes.

The cyber pandemic is just the same. We do not have the cyber resources on deck or in the wings to meet the global demand and fight these threats. It is estimated that there are three million cyber positions open in the U.S.A. Alongside the demand internationally, it will be nearly ten million by the year 2023.

So why do you care? We have lots of technology, we are spending lots of money, and if we are hit, it is the security and I.T.s problem; they failed! That is a comfortable bedtime story to hide behind, but let's face reality.

Now that we have acknowledged that we are in the middle of a cyber pandemic, we have many levels of attack vectors that need to be covered. With the biological pandemic on reset, we have a global workforce network that is trying to balance when and where one can access data to do their job. We have greater tools, but so do the bad actors.

In 2020, we adapted to a model that most people were working from home; we updated their technology, as well as VPN and role-based authentication. It was not perfect, but it provided a layer of protection because, in most cases, we had a better understanding of our landscape.

In 2021, lots of us are going back, and all will be good – full stop – we are now back in an even greater hybrid model, as we have people coming into our facilities with greater access. Then we have people who are also working from home on off days and are able to work from more locations, as they are not open. So our landscape has changed again, and humans are now a greater risk to our data and systems, as they are laxer, so we need to focus quickly on the training.

Going back to the biological pandemic process of distancing, hand washing and masks need to be re-communicated to the workforce quickly – scenario training is key; add a prize for the people who get it correct. That expense is less than ransomware.

Ransomware is used by malicious actors to target an individual or organization to extort a ransom from them. It is a set of tools that encrypts the data, systems, and/or tools, making that data inaccessible. Without advance planning, the only option a target of ransomware has is to pay the ransom, typically with cryptocurrency, to restore access to their data.

A malicious actor (internal or external) trolls for a way to access the network or individual devices, such as:

1. WAN/LAN/cloud/mobile vulnerabilities.

2. Social engineering tactics such as phishing.
3. Access via a stolen or lost device.
4. Current or legacy technology not wiped prior to disposal.
5. Disgruntled contractor or employee.

The malicious actor circumvents or disables the network or system's antivirus protection software. They open a 'backdoor,' either something that was coded in the past or a new operation that was installed when the anti-virus software was no longer enabled. They can then utilize other vulnerabilities to escalate access to more systems' privileges. The malicious actor then gains full control over the network or devices and can steal data or install malware, such as ransomware. In the case of ransomware, the actor then tries to extort the company/individual into paying to restore data and access to the systems.

However, even if the company does resort to payment, there is no guarantee that access will be restored or that other backdoors or malware won't be left behind. Malicious actors target all operating systems (OS), including BYOD (bring your own device), phones, or professional services automation systems. The days of Microsoft OS being a sole target are gone.

What is next? – The bad actors are testing the waters from the state-sponsored teams, and so are the dark-web teams and the person in his or her mom's basement. The saying is true; idle hands are the devil's workshop.

Let's review the data.

Ransomware has been in existence for over 30 years, and ransom has been paid to the bad actors over the same time period, so why has it now become the main topic?

The media is a large player in this. Social media is a major player. There is greater transparency of how data is being managed, from GDPR to laws on the books to laws pending around the world, to give people more access and control to how their PII data is being managed.

The new technology comes into play here. Not only do we have people of all types and skills trying to play the game, but we also now have machine learning, as Artificial Intelligence is moving into the game. Remember, just like people, we will have all levels of ML/AI trying to play the game. Up until now, the games had been money; perceived scare tactics. But the trigger of WWD is just around the corner. The stakes are getting higher, and the ethics between thieves are getting very slim. At any given time, just listen to the players on the dark web; they joke, play off each other's ability, share ideas and even go to the rescue of a common goal that makes them look more like Robin Hood rather than Lord Voldemort. The tide is changing; the conversations are more about trying to combine with each other, looking at bigger targets, and causing greater impact and carnage.

Think of 9/11 on steroids or the Fukushima Daiichi nuclear disaster caused by someone besides Mother Nature. Is it hard to imagine? No, it is not. The current and next generations are playing out what they see as real-life scenarios in all of the war games, and all the militaries want the individuals that not only are sanitized to the impact but have wired their brains for faster and more accurate eye-hand coordination. Driving the next generations of super-tech geeks is easier than you think. But morality will always be our counter, and good over evil will always be victorious. Well, that story has been playing out for over 4,000 years, from sticks and stones to IADs and other WMDs, and we still have them against us. But the rules are changing, the bounty is greater, and the impact could last for the next 4,000 years.

Not possible, you say. Well, answer this question: what set of actions could put the earth back into the dark ages in weeks, not years, and it would only take a few lines of code and access to old OS's? I am not going to put the answer in this book, but it is something to think about – a few hints: it is not nuclear; it is not biological; it is not alien-ware, but we depend on it for everything we do, and, without it, within weeks, the social and political bases around the world will collapse.

So how do we counter the ongoing events and try to find a balance of power within the cyber pandemic?

Simple answer: we cooperate on the layers of defense. Not one company or person has a silver bullet. As I have said before, many will try to sell you that story.

What are the layers in defense?

Let's start with you.

Do you take personal security as a priority?

Have you ever talked to your family, friends, or coworkers about security?

Have you ever asked your children's teachers if they talk about it in school?

Would any of the school staff have a clue, assuming the fifth-grader knows more?

Who do you think is responsible for protection? The government, the companies, the schools, the apps you use, the sites you access, the technology interaction you have with IOT, or you?

The answer is, all of them, and each of them has its own strengths and weaknesses.

Yes, we do not have time to think about this, but we need

to learn. We all know from a young age that a stove is hot, that a rock will hurt, and a cut needs to be cleaned, so you do not get infected. Yet, we have massive groups of people around the world that are not taking the vaccine seriously, so they are exposing all of us to the next level, but they can justify it through incorrect data and lack of knowledge just to prove that they are right, and everyone else is wrong.

Let's get real. If I wanted to install a chip in you to track or control your mind, I would put it in the junk food and soda you drink at an alarming level. Mass-producing this would increase the level of success that it was ingested and lodged somewhere in your body.

Let's review the layers of defense:

1) Training – Within any technology system, the greatest vulnerability is the humans involved. Companies need to train and communicate the risks to individuals, outlining clear work-from-home do's and don'ts to limit unauthorized access to networks, systems, and data. What are the ways the bad actors can influence you – anything that connects to anything can be modified in a good or bad way:
    a. Social media
    b. Social engineering

c. Old-school trickery
d. E-mail
e. Paper letters
f. Websites
g. Apps
h. IOT products you attached to your device
i. NFC
j. RFID
k. Scanning via your phone
l. Open or weak Wi-Fi
m. Free Wi-Fi offers
n. Power ports
o. Portal power pacts.

2) Layers of defense:

a. User and family training
b. AV tools – need to be up to date
c. OS updates – no matter how many you need to perform
d. Phase phrases – not a password
e. Mobile phones – all the same tools you have on your PC
f. Home routers
g. Business-provided routers
h. Always use a VPN

i. Never share your business computer
j. Load only business-only apps
k. Companies should require a password to be able to load an app or device. It is a pain, but it is a layer of defense that works.
l. Role-based authentication
m. Secondary dual-factor authentication
n. Separate corporation and guest Wi-Fi
o. Fully segmented networks from production, R&D, test, lab…
p. Monitoring tools
    i. Facilities' entrance and exit.
    ii. Network
        1. Printer
        2. Fax
        3. …
    iii. Servers
    iv. Applications
    v. Mobile apps
q. Ease of escalation
    i. 0365 notifications
    ii. Gmail notifications
r. Cloud Services
    i. Who is charging in what to AP

ii. Understanding what or who has third-party accounts

One layer of the security stack companies often overlook, called on-premise data management, is removable. These systems are in operation in tens of thousands of systems globally daily. These systems are being leveraged to back up, store and distribute data across a wide spectrum of markets, including healthcare, manufacturing, marketing, training, military, and government. These systems provide low-cost, fast access to recorded data. This is critical to start rebuilding your data baseline as an event is unfolding.

It's impossible to prevent attacks with 100% success. That's why it's critical to have a comprehensive data security strategy that allows you to back up, store, and archive your data in multiple formats and locations. One of the key elements of the data-security toolset is removable, on-premises data management. Organizations should look for a removable, on-premises data-management solution with a global reach, a proven track record, and a commitment to continuous innovation.

Chapter 3

Cyber Attacks

Cyber-attacks become more and more a daily reality for both companies of all sizes and single individuals. However, very little is universally known about cyber-crime. M. Uma and G. Padmavathi (2013) outline a general lack of understanding of the different types of attacks, characteristics, and possible results, which may pose an obstacle in defending information security. Several definitions of the terms cyber-attack, cyber-crime, etc., can be found among the international literature, all having in a common aim to compromise the confidentiality, integrity, and data availability.

The technological evolution also brings along cybercrime progress; thus, new ways to perform attacks that reach even harder-to-penetrate targets and remain untracked are developed continuously. However, traditional cyber threats remain the source of the most common attacks. Various types of attacks have been defined and studied among the international literature:

- 'Man in the middle' attack occurs when the attacker interferes between the two communication ends. Thus, every message sent from source A to source B reaches the attacker before reaching its destination. The risks further posed by this type of attack comprise of unauthorized access to sensitive information or the possibility to alter the information/message that reaches the destination by the attacker.

- Brute force attack comprises of repeated attempts to gain access to protected information (e.g., passwords, encryption, etc.) until the correct key is found, and information can thus be reached).
- DDoS (Distributed Denial of Service) is a type of attack that compromises the availability of data, in a way that the attacker floods the victim (e.g., server) with commands, thus becoming inoperable.
- Malware is a generic term describing types of malicious software used by the attacker to compromise the confidentiality, availability, and integrity of data. The most common types of malware are viruses, worms, Trojans, spyware, ransomware, adware, and scareware/rogware.
- Phishing is a technique aiming to steal private information from users by masquerading as a trustful source (e.g., a website).

- Social engineering is the general term that describes techniques used to gain unauthorized access to information through human interaction.

Price Water house Cooper's study, The Global State of Information Security 2015, outlines the fact that cyber-crime has developed to the extent that brings over 117,000 attacks per day.

The study commenced with a careful review of cyber-crime's current position by reviewing specialized international literature, including legal aspects and analysis of the last years' significant events. The aim was to gain a general overview of the cyber-attacks from all over the world, understand the means of operating and potential impact on businesses or individuals, and the countermeasures to be taken for addressing the risks. The research was based on attacks identified and traced over the last three years.

Given the significant number of cyber-attacks undertaken daily all around the world, as well as the limited information companies usually display when they are the victim of cyber-crime, and the fact that some attacks are brutal to be traced, it was impossible for the authors to gain a complete set of data for analysis purposes. However, the study was based on the information resulting from aggregating data regarding attacks detected and traced throughout the last three years, collected from news and attacks history, as well as from reports and surveys issued by globally major market players in security consulting and anti-malware services, thus, reaching a population of over 15 million attacks.

The study was based on a population of over 15 million attacks, collected throughout news and events, as well as reported by major players in the industry of security and consulting: Cenzic, CISCO, FBI (Federal Bureau of Investigations), Fire Eye, Kaspersky, McAfee, Mandiant, Sophos, Symantec, Verizon, Price Waterhouse Coopers, and hackmageddon.com.

McAfee Labs' report, Threats Predictions 2015, supports the idea that cyber-attack will pursue an increasing trend, outlining the expectancy of increased espionage and cyber-warfare, also strengthened by hackers' improved strategies and tools for hiding their identity/location and obtaining sensitive data. According to the report, 'Attacks on Internet-of-Things devices will increase rapidly due to hyper growth in the number of connected objects, poor security hygiene, and the high value of data on IoT devices,' also forecasting an estimated number of 50 billion devices to be connected to the internet by 2019. In addition, the results outline the fact that attackers continuously develop new ways to exploit networks, programs, and data. One other trend that has been noted is the continuous increase of mobile attacks from one year to another.

An interesting fact that the study reveals is that, looking at the root cause of the security breaches, less than 50% of the cases are due to criminal-intended attacks, the causes being split between three factors: the intended attack, the human error, and the system vulnerabilities. The results outline the fact that when an attack succeeds, it is only partly due to the attacker's skills and knowledge and also due to vulnerabilities from the victim's side – that is, faulty programs, human errors, or insufficient level of controls to ensure information security. In 2013, Cenzic Company detected one or more major security vulnerabilities in 96% of the analyzed applications, according to the 2014 Application Vulnerability Trends Report, with a median of 14 vulnerabilities per application.

Throughout the study, it was hard to determine the exact number or percentage of different attack types. However, the most common attacks are denial of service, malicious codes, viruses, worms and Trojans, malware, malicious insiders, stolen devices, phishing and social engineering, and web-based attacks.

With regards to the impact that cyber-attacks have upon their victims, it is hard, if not impossible, to quantify the exact costs that organizations require for recovering their businesses, customers' trust, and image, especially considering that companies do not always reveal all information to the public. However, the results show that the impact of cyber-attacks most often concerns the loss of information, business disruption, revenue loss, and equipment damage. The most common types of attacks granted unauthorized access to information comprising: full names, birth dates, personal IDs, full addresses, medical records, phone numbers, financial data, e-mail addresses, credentials (usernames, passwords), and insurance information.

What are some of the unexpected costs of a ransomware attack?

There are two primary focus areas when it comes to unexpected malicious attacks: sociological impact and internal culture.

- **Sociological** – with all the WFH, remote training, and uncommunicated training on do's and don'ts on handling x-ware attacks, survey results show fatigue. The follow-through is not as good. People want to know why they are on the front line vs. the technology. The messages, not unlike the Mask messages, are different. Companies outline policy and direction, schools outline a different approach, and each institution that a person interacts with also has a different version of a security policy. In parallel, inspect the cultural view if you are doing business globally.

- **Internal Culture** – a company's communication and follow-up need to be grounded in a 'we are in this together' approach and thinking about how we can help each other. Raise your hand, as no question is a dumb question while we are amid a cyber pandemic with no foreseeable end in sight.

Lots of the focus is on lost business, recovery, ransom paid, consultant fees, etc.

- Companies need to take a three-pronged approach when addressing malicious attacks and trying to prevent them.

- Leadership communication expressing being proactive is critical.

- Outline what ransom and x-ware are and how these attacks can damage the company.

- Outline the approach the company is taking and how they need to be a part of the actions. Many companies have employees, contractors, or vendors posting things on social media. This can show up as screenshots of the ransomware message or the 'dumb' process the company makes them do. Humans are the weakest link. If the company is hit with a malicious attack, the recovery may not happen, and appropriate cuts, like process and people, may occur.

But perhaps less understood are direct and indirect costs, such as higher insurance fees, investments in marketing and PR to rebuild reputation, and added expenses from closer security vetting by partners.

- One of the main takeaways is working with your insurance broker and the companies that are a part of your policies (most have more than one).
- These discussions should have IT, security, CFO, and CEO-level participation. Everyone needs to understand the impact. If you have a policy but do not use it, then insurance will not pay. After an event, the insurance companies prepare with full due diligence to ensure you have followed the processes, the training, and the actions if an employee did not follow directions.
- This is also cascading down to all your vendors and suppliers. If they connect to your environment, send you emails, or share .ftp files, then you need to have complete processes in place. On a global basis, this is a management process that is a significant gap, as many companies do not have this in place.

- Understanding the impact can also be a massive PR effort. A lot of companies look at PR from a disaster recovery lens. This is important to incorporate your internal culture and your customers' data health in your business continuity process. Continued discussions with your clients will allow your process to flourish regardless of direct or indirect impact. Regardless of industry or region, this process can be somewhat fluid as the dangers mature and your approach progresses.

Please share your thoughts on some of these—as well as others you're aware of—such as how much these other costs can come to, how common they are, etc.

The biggest takeaway is that you need to understand your data flow and ownership

- Where is your data stored?
- If you were breached, what can they get to?
- If they got to some of the data, how would you react?

Perform tabletop exercises with your teams, leadership, and vendors. This will take time, but in the long run, it might save you more than just time.

Here are some essential housekeeping items:

- Your data flow
- Role-based authentication
- Password management
- Segregation of duties (in house and externally)
- Locking down the ability to not install or load apps without admin approval (this can be challenging for most but will pay off dividends if and when you are attacked)
- Real discussion and training with your teams
- How things are entered into the system
- How being connected from home has risks
- Why they need to always have a VPN running
- Not letting their kids use their PC to do homework and not connecting to the schools' network
- When someone fails a test email or process, they are not to be called out – you should work with them to understand the driver, as this needs to go back into the training.

Generational Discussions

- Most executives, even the CISO, CIO, and CTO, are from the flip-phone generation. We are not up to date, but the new generations do not grasp the impact. BYD, always on social media, trading apps, and games with everyone, needing to be online all the time, and not thinking about the company. Have a corporate network, a guest network, a mobile network, and if you have an open work process, then have the gaming and social access through a VPN that keeps everything away from the production network.
- If you have a disgruntled or released employee, contractor, VAR (value-added reseller), or supplier, make sure they have disconnected ASAP even if this is a hardship – you have no control and limited recourse. After the damage is done, in some time, it will not matter.
- The biggest takeaway is that this is a cyber pandemic; it will never go away, not all the money in the world will fix it, and all the tools will be broken at some time. Think about what needs to be offline, what needs to be available, and what can be a request. You need to reset expectations and remember this is

> global, and everyone is at risk. You may be a small provider of something in the overall supply chain. If I can figure that out and can lock you down, I do not need to get money from you, but I will go upstream and get money from the guys with money. This is not only state-sponsored, revenge-driven, just because – this is the new underbelly of the dark web, and all data is for sale.

In today's day and age, we have formally entered WWD/3, with the fall of Afghanistan and Taiwan officially recognizing that the war they are fighting is cyber-based. Setting all politics aside, these events, being parallel to the biological and cyber pandemics we are in and will be in our lifetime, we need to understand the drivers and how this will impact us and our businesses. Every day, we read about a new cyber-attack and a new outbreak of the Delta variant, and, yes, we will have many more versions of both x-ware, ransomware, and biological-driven variants.

Let us think of the six levels of separation. With each variant, the global supply chain is impacted, the global economy is impacted, and this directly flows down from the company you work for to the products you buy and the food you put on your table. The cost impact on your pocketbook is also direct. Let us touch on a few – the price of fuel on a global basis was struggling due to the reduced use, and over the past few months, this has removed to 70+ dollars per barrel. Now, after the fall of Afghanistan, the global oil supply chain has started to take on risks as the possibility of increased unrest in the region escalates. This cascades down to the companies trying to move the products. Global shipping demand cannot be met; the cost of a container is now 250% of what it was three months ago. So, why do you care?

We now have 38.4 million people in Afghanistan that do not like us. Of that number, you have about 10% that are trained in the cyber field. So, do the math. We think the Chinese and Russians and the guys and girls in their mother's basement are a risk. Little are we aware that we now have people that want to kill us, not just take out services and prove they can. This will not happen tomorrow, but as with the systematic overthrow of each city in Afghanistan, a bunch of thugs on camels did not accomplish this. This has a robust set of leadership with a lot of insider information. Do not think only of the economic impact on your daily life but also on you and your life directly. What can they do? They can cause planes to fall from the sky and cause trains carrying major chemicals to crash. They can cause self-driving cars to become rockets into buildings, traffic, schools, etc. The capability is there today; they just need to focus on the task at hand.

Step back again and ask yourself what the biological or cyber impact is, the next generation of an engineered virus or a cyber-attack? We are all in this together, so we all need to take responsibility to address this. When you need to download an app, is it safe? Do your children understand the risks? Well, I am not sure I can help with it. To accomplish any protection, you need layers of defense. Just like the biological events, you need distance, masks, washing hands, vaccinations, etc. With the cyber pandemic, you need to be vigilant. Like in WW2, loose lips sink ships, and Hitler was always listening. Now, the bad actors are watching your e-mail, v-mail, trash, and tracking the bad apps you downloaded or the open Wi-Fi you connected to – remember, you need to trust but verify.

Chapter 4

Patterns and Effects

In comparing cybercrime with conventional crime, there is not much difference because both cause breaching of legal rules. Hackers can expose your personal information or even shut down your entire business operations for hours or days. Security deficiencies are costing for-profit and non-profit organizations billions of dollars in losses. Plus, with companies shifting to remote work since the pandemic began, they have become more vulnerable to attacks from hackers.

Cyberattacks are now the fastest-growing crime on a global scale. Financial losses from cybercrime exceed the total losses incurred from the global trade of all illegal drugs; losses are estimated at 10 billion dollars annually. Hence, it comes as no surprise that individuals and organizations operating on the web live in fear of potential hacking scenarios and data breaches. Aside from financial losses, such forms of cyber-attacks can lead to reputation damage as well. Consumer data, when compromised, can subject businesses to strict regulations and costly settlements.

Half of these cyberattacks are targeting small businesses that usually don't have sufficient cybersecurity measures to protect themselves from such threats. Based on a 2020 survey, the most common cyber-attacks experienced by US companies are phishing (38%), network intrusion (32%), inadvertent disclosure (12%), stolen/lost device or records (8%), and system misconfiguration (5%) (BakerHostetler, 2020[1]).

Even though cybercrime is at its peak, the majority of the population is unaware of most cyberattack methods. A report by Infosec indicates that about 97% of the people in the world cannot identify a phishing email, while 1 in 25 people click such emails, thus, falling prey to cyberattacks (Infosec[2]).

According to a few facts and figures from the 2016 Norton Cyber Security Insights Report[3], 40% of millennials reported having experienced cybercrime in the past year. Nearly three in ten people cannot detect a phishing attack. Another 13% have to guess between a real message and a phishing email, meaning four in ten are vulnerable. 86% of people said they may have experienced a phishing incident, and seven in ten consumers

---

[1] (BakerHostetler. (2020, April). *2020 Data Security Incident Response Report*. BakerHostetler)

[2] (Dimov, I. (2017, August 29). *Security awareness statistics*. Infosec)

[3] https://us.norton.com/internetsecurity-emerging-threats-personal-impact-cybercrime.html

wish they could make their home Wi-Fi network more secure. Yet only 27% believe it is likely their home Wi-Fi network could be compromised.

These days, nearly everyone uses smart mobile devices—66.6% of the world population as of 2021, to be specific (DataReportal, 2021[4]). Most leading ecommerce software and platforms are accessible through mobile platforms.

The number of connected devices has exponentially grown in the last year, and there is a constant need to be connected. In fact, people are willing to engage in risky online behavior in order to simply access Wi-Fi. People are also known to share their passwords with friends, access financial information via unsecured Wi-Fi connections, and click on suspicious links, thereby increasing the vulnerability of their connected devices.

Cybercriminals, however, see this as an opportunity to target mobile users and use mobile devices as attack vectors. Mobile devices are becoming a great channel of opportunity for cybercriminals as users continue to use their mobile devices for personal and business communications, as well as banking, shopping, flight, or hotel bookings. These devices became targets

---

[4] (DataReportal, Hootsuite, & We Are Social. (2021, January). *Global digital overview*. DataReportal)

of cyberattacks.

80% of the consumers who took a compromising action in response to a potential phishing incident experienced negative consequences, including identify theft, money stolen from bank accounts, credit cards opened in their name, and unauthorized apps installed on their device[5]. According to the RSA's 2019 Current State of Cybercrime whitepaper, about 70% of fraudulent transactions originated from mobile platforms, with popular mobile attack vectors including malware, data tampering, and data loss (RSA, 2019[6]).

"Your entire life, from the intimate to the mundane, is becoming increasingly digital, and your digital information may be uniquely accessible to a worldwide audience of potential perpetrators. The more this digitization becomes ubiquitous and standard, the more you may be prone to disregarding the inherent risks as society as a whole is lulled into complacency. In fact, a Pew Research study determined that many Internet users cannot correctly answer more than half the questions on a cybersecurity quiz."[7]

---

[5] https://us.norton.com/internetsecurity-emerging-threats-personal-impact-cybercrime.html

[6] (RSA. (2019). *2019 current state of cybercrime*. RSA)

[7] https://www.uagc.edu/blog/how-cybercrime-affects-society

Apart from this, cybercriminals now resort to more advanced and high-tech forms of phishing and malware infections. According to Shea (2012), cybercriminals have used various channels to distribute illegal emails and websites and commit simple crimes such as downloading illegal music files. Wall (2007) posits that international criminals steal intellectual property for their own or at the request of their governments. Germany, for example, estimated its own IP losses from industrial espionage at 25–50 billion dollars, much of which is caused by weak internet security.

Wall (2007) argues that cybercrime has not created new crimes but has, instead, provided an additional method through which offenses such as theft, extortion, illegal protests, and terrorism thrive. According to Moore (2016), terrorism in cyberspace takes many forms, such as physical destruction of machinery, remote interference of computer networks, disruption of government networks, and mass media. A good example of such destruction is from 2015, when an alleged Russian cyber attacker seized control of the Prykarpatnergo Control Center (PCC) in Western Ukraine. This incident left approximately 230,000 people without power for up to six hours! Here are a few other instances where cybercrime affected entire countries:

- India's national centralized government ID database (Aadhaar), which stores the biometric data (i.e., thumbprints and iris scans) and identity data of 1.2 billion Indians, and is used to verify nationals' identities for financial, government, utilities, and other services, was subjected to a database breach in 2018, resulting in the compromise of identity data, such as access names, 12-digit identity numbers, phone numbers, email addresses, and postal codes, but not the biometric data (Safi, 2018[8]; Doshi, 2018[9]).

- The information of approximately 30 million South Africans was leaked online in 2017, including their names, genders, income, employment history, identity numbers, phone numbers, and home addresses, because of a data breach suffered by one of the top real estate companies in the country, Jigsaw Holdings (Fihlani, 2017[10]; Gous, 2017[11]).
- Over three billion Yahoo users' data was compromised in 2013, including names, email

---

[8] (Safi, Michael. (2018). Personal data of a billion Indians sold online for £6, report claims. *The Guardian*, 4 January, 2018)

[9] (Vidhi Doshi. (2018). A security breach in India has left a billion people at risk of identity theft. *The Washington Post*, 4 January 2018)

[10] (Fihlani, Pumza, (2017). Millions caught in South Africa's 'worst data breach '. *BBC News*, 20 October 2017)

[11] (Gous, Nico. (2017). Top real estate company admits to being unwitting source of country's largest personal data breach. *Sunday Times*, 18 October 2017)

addresses, passwords (with encryption that could be easily bypassed), and birth dates (Newman, 2017[12]).

- Deloitte, a global consulting firm, was accessed through an unsecured account, compromising the usernames and passwords, among other information, of approximately 350 clients (Hopkins, 2017[13]).
- The personal data (i.e., national identifier, name, gender, parents' names, home address, date of birth, and city of birth) of over 49 million Turkish citizens were made available in 2016 through an online searchable database (Greenberg, 2016[14]).
- The personal and biometric data of over 55 million voters in the Philippines were compromised in 2016 after black hat hackers gained unauthorized access to the Commission of Election (COMELEC) website (Tan, 2016[15]).

Notably, most enterprises do not report harm from cybercrimes, indicating that the figure could be higher. Other

---

[12] (Newman, Lily Hay. (2017). Yahoo's 2013 email hack actually compromised three billion accounts. *Wired,* 3 October 2017)

[13] (Hopkins, Nick. (2017). Deloitte hack hit server containing emails from across US government. *The Guardian*, 10 October 2017)

[14] (Greenberg, Andy. (2016). Hack brief: Turkey breach spills info on more than half its citizens. *Wired*, 5 April 2016)

[15] (Tan, Lara. (2016). 55M Filipino voters open to fraud after Comelec hack - int'l tech security firm. *CNN Philippines*, 8 April 2016)

companies that have been hacked choose to conceal the information to avert scaring customers and investors.

Phishing attacks are currently the most pervasive security threat to the IT sector, with many still falling victim to phishing emails. Since cybercriminals use more advanced methods to create well-executed business email compromise attacks (BEC), phishing emails and malicious URLs remain prevalent on the web, except that they are now highly localized, more personalized, and are geo-targeted.

According to the 2019 Data Breach Investigations Report of Verizon, 32% of the data breaches last year involved phishing activities (NIST 2019[16]). Thus, experts see targeted phishing becoming more prevalent in the coming years. It is also important to note that 2020 alone saw more than 60,000 phishing websites, and one in every eight employees shares information on a phishing site (Security Boulevard, 2020[17]).

In the healthcare sector, failing to combat cyber threats exposes many individuals and organizations to all sorts of liability and security issues. This led to hospitals and health organizations investing more in cybersecurity.

---

[16] (Widdup, S. (2019). *2019 Verizon Data Breach Investigations Report*. NIST)

[17] (Meharchandani, D. (2020, December 7). *Staggering phishing statistics in 2020*. Security Boulevard)

In 2019, the value of the healthcare cybersecurity market was $9.78 billion, which is projected to rise to $33.65 billion by 2027 (GlobeNewswire, 2020[18]). Considering the impact of COVID-19 on the healthcare sector, experts predict that the market might reach $125 billion as early as 2025 (Cybersecurity Ventures, 2020[19]).

Data breaches are among the leading cybersecurity threats in healthcare. From 2015 to 2019, 157.40 million healthcare records were exposed (Healthcare, 2020[20]). According to IBM, data breaches like this in the healthcare industry cost organizations an average of $7.13 million in 2020 (IBM, 2020[21]).

Regardless, amid the Coronavirus outbreak, some healthcare organizations temporarily relaxed their firewall rules to make it easier for staff to work from home. Many also needed to expand telehealth services and erect temporary medical facilities that bypassed some of the security diligence protocols

---

[18] (Fior Market Research LLP. (2020, September 30). *Global healthcare cyber security market is expected to reach USD 33.65 billion by 2027: Fior Markets*. GlobeNewswire)

[19] (Morgan, S. (2020, September 8). *Healthcare industry to spend $125 billion on cybersecurity from 2020 to 2025*. Cybercrime Magazine)

[20] (Seh, A. H., Zarour, M., Alenezi, M., Sarkar, A. K., Agrawal, A., Kumar, R., & Ahmad Khan, R. (2020). Healthcare data breaches: Insights and implications. *Healthcare, 8*(2), 133)

[21] (IBM. (2020, July 29). *IBM report: Compromised employee accounts led to most expensive data breaches over past year*. IBM)

of vendors or lacked the usual security infrastructure present in established hospitals.

These figures show that cyberattacks in the healthcare sector are far from being stopped. Data breaches present a continuing threat to health organizations as sensitive information about businesses, employees, and patients remains the top target of cybercriminals. According to a survey by the law firm BakerHostetler, US health systems and hospitals account for about a quarter of cyberattacks in the country.

In July of 2019, an Alabama baby was born with severe brain injury and eventually died due to botched care because her hospital was struggling with a ransomware attack[22]. The filing was the first credible public claim that someone's death was caused at least in part by hackers who remotely shut down hospital computers in an extortion attempt, a rising trend in cybercrime.

The lawsuit, filed by Teiranni Kidd, the baby's mother, was first reported by The Wall Street Journal. It alleged that the hospital, Springhill Medical Center, didn't tell her that hospital computer were down because of a cyberattack and subsequently gave her severely diminished care when she arrived to deliver her

---

[22] https://www.nbcnews.com/news/baby-died-due-ransomware-attack-hospital-suit-claims-rcna2465

daughter.

Springhill announced in 2019 that it had been the victim of a 'network security incident,' a common euphemism for a cyberattack. As reported at the time by local news station WKRG, Springhill claimed to be seeing a regular volume of patients at the time, even though it was turning some away because of the ransomware attack.

Kidd initially sued the hospital in 2019, then amended the lawsuit that July after her daughter died. According to the lawsuit, Kidd wasn't informed Springhill was struggling with a cyberattack when she went in to deliver her daughter. Doctors and nurses then missed a few key tests that would have shown that the umbilical cord was wrapped around the baby's neck, leading to brain damage and death nine months later.

Ransomware, where hackers lock up a victim's computers and demand payment for a program to make them usable again, is a surging, multi-billion-dollar worldwide cybercriminal industry. Around 850 healthcare networks and hospitals in the US have been affected by the ransomware so far this year alone, said Allan Liska, a ransomware analyst at the cybersecurity company Recorded Future.

Cybersecurity experts particularly worry about attacks on healthcare facilities, which can be quickly thrown into disarray if their computer networks go down. For years, they've grimly waited for the milestone of the first confirmed death due to a hospital ransomware attack.

"It's an awful thing, but we've been expecting this for years to happen, because when things go wrong, eventually somebody's going to die," Liska said.

In another instance, a German woman died in 2020 after being rerouted to a different emergency room because the closest hospital was hit with ransomware. But government authorities later found there wasn't sufficient evidence that the ransomware played a key role in her death.

Coming to the education sector, in 2019, three private universities fell victim to a cyberattack that involved the hacking of student admission data (Inside Higher Ed, 2019[23]). This called the attention of those in the higher education sector to actively promote tighter security for the protection of student, faculty, and research data in the institution.

Security Scorecard's 2018 Education Cybersecurity Report pointed out that in terms of cybersecurity, education comes in last out of the 17 industries in the US (Security

---

[23] (Jaschik, S. (2019, March 11). *Three private colleges have admissions files hacked.* Inside Higher Ed)

Scorecard[24]). Furthermore, the report indicates that the higher education sector performed poorly in patching cadence, network security, and application security. This is even more alarming, as 11% of attacks on US educational institutions are motivated by espionage (Verizon, 2019[25]).

The financial services sector is another industry facing cyber threats daily and has been increasingly targeted by cybercriminals. They tend to go after Automated Teller Machines, credit cards, and online bank accounts. In a single example, a Russian gang took $9.8 million from ATMs over a Labor Day weekend. The cybercrime threat has become widespread, touching on all corners of the globe and affecting developmental efforts socially and economically.

It also doesn't help that some financial organizations are still struggling to keep pace with cloud migration and the increasing number of regulations. Phishing attacks remain prevalent in the financial services sector, but it's no longer just via emails. Phishing through social media and other messaging platforms is now among the cybersecurity trends in financial services.

---

[24] (SecurityScorecard. (2018). *2018 education cybersecurity report*. SecurityScorecard)

[25] (Verizon. (2019, May 7). *Data breaches in educational services*. Verizon)

Aside from phishing attacks, the most common threats faced by insurance companies, banks, and asset managers include malware attacks and data breaches. A report by Boston Consulting Group revealed that financial services firms are 300 times more prone to cybersecurity attacks than businesses in other industries (BCG, 2019[26]).

Moreover, cyber-attacks on financial institutions spiked by a massive 238% from the beginning of February to the end of April 2020 amid the COVID-19 pandemic (Infosecurity Magazine, 2020[27]), and attacks now cost the banking industry $18.3 million per enterprise (Security Boulevard, 2020[28]).

Outside of breaches, medical, financial, and other personal data could be found on dedicated online carding forums (i.e., online sites dedicated to selling debit and credit card data) and darknet sites (located on the Deep Web).

In addition to releasing this data for financial purposes, compromised data can (and has) been released to shame people and expose their real or perceived immoral actions and behaviors.

---

[26] (BCG. (2019, June 20). *For wealth managers, off year sparks opportunity to reignite growth.* BCG)

[27] (Muncaster, P. (2020, May 15). *Attacks on banks spike 238% during #COVID19 crisis.* Infosecurity Magazine)

[28] (Singha, R. (2020, December 19). B*anking industry faces surge in cyber security challenges.* Security Boulevard)

A case in point is the posting of the personal information (e.g., names and email addresses) of approximately 37 million users of Ashley Madison. This website connected users seeking extramarital affairs online (Zetter, 2015)[29].

Cybercrime violates individuals' privacy and the security of their data, particularly hacking, malware, identity theft, financial fraud, medical fraud, and certain offenses against persons that involve the revealing of personal information, messages, images, and video and audio recordings without individuals' consent or permission (e.g., cyberstalking, cyber-harassment, and cyberbullying. These fall under interpersonal cybercrimes).

'Interpersonal cybercrimes' refers to those cybercrimes committed by individuals against other individuals with whom they are interacting, communicating, and/or having some form of real or imagined relationship (Maras, 2016[30]). There can be one or more perpetrators of interpersonal cybercrime targeting one or more victims anywhere in the world with an internet connection, making the policing of such crimes particularly complicated

---

[29] https://www.unodc.org/e4j/en/cybercrime/module-10/key-issues/cybercrime-that-compromises-privacy.html

[30] (Maras, Marie-Helen. (2016). *Cybercriminology*. University Press)

(Henry, Flynn and Powell, 2018[31]).

Interpersonal cybercrime can have significant adverse psychological, social, political (depending on the person's position), and economic impacts on victims, including (but not limited to) stress, fear, anxiety, depression, shame, loss of social standing, and reputational harm, loss of human dignity, personal autonomy, and privacy, and financial burden from medical and counseling services, legal support, and online protection services and software and offline security measures (Williford, et al., 2013[32]; Marcum, Higgins, and Ricketts, 2014[33]; UNODC, 2015[34]; Maras, 2016[35]). Furthermore, there have been many instances of interpersonal cybercrime in various parts of the

---

[31] Henry, Nicola, Flynn, Asher and Powell, Anastasia. (2018). Policing Image-based Sexual Abuse: Stakeholder Perspectives. *Police Practice and Research: An International Journal*,Vol. 19(6), 565-581

[32] (Williford, Anne, Lawrence Christian Elledge, Aaron J. Boulton, Kathryn J. DePaolis, Todd D. Little, and Christina Salmivalli. (2013). Effects of the KiVa Antibullying Program on Cyberbullying and Cybervictimization Frequency Among Finnish Youth. *Journal of Clinical Child & Adolescent Psychology*, Vol. 42(6), 820-833)

[33] (Marcum, Catherine D., Geroge E. Higgins, and Melissa L. Ricketts. (2014). Juveniles and Cyber Stalking in the United States: An Analysis of Theoretical Predictors of Patterns of Online Perpetration. *International Journal of Cyber Criminology*, No. 8(1), 47-56)

[34] (UNODC. (2015). *Study on the Effects of New Information Technologies on the Abuse and Exploitation of Children*)

[35] (Maras, Marie-Helen. (2016). *Cybercriminology*. University Press)

world where victims have committed suicide in response to these cybercrimes. These cybercrimes, therefore, require special attention not only because their impacts on victims are severe but also because, in many cases, their consequences are irreversible.

Keeping that in mind, within the past year, cybercrime victims have spent $126 billion globally and lost 19.7 hours – the time it would take to fly from New York City to Los Angeles four times – dealing with cybercrime!

As you finish the book, take a few minutes to ask yourself, *"What can I do to help?"* This book takes on the question of how the cyber pandemic is changing the way you think, your work, and the way you live, just as the biological pandemic is doing. If we ignore either of them, they will not go away, and we will lose people we care for.

As with the biological pandemic, the cyber pandemic is slowly causing the loss of life. It is still in the shadows; one mishap here, one system failure there, but sometime soon, a major event will occur, and we will all stand around as with 9/11 and ask how that could happen. All the cyberwar engines will go into mutation to block and track down who did it.

So, setting all politics aside, remember that the leaders around the world, and their advisors, are from the flip phone era; they do not understand how fast technology is changing. So, asking open questions to these leaders is not wrong as your children will be inheriting the world. So, again – history continues to repeat itself. Still, we do not have a technology history of building upon, so when we allow the cyber pandemic history to be written, we are the authors and have no one else to blame.

To add insult to injury, all data you put in the cloud will always be found. No company, tool, or system can erase any or all your data. We can put all the privacy laws and processes into place and can even add massive penalties. Still, someone, somewhere, has made some backup, some replication tool, some failed batch job, or someone with access made a copy just for fun, so all systems retain some part of your data. So, when they want to classify you or find you, they can. But most of us are not worth the effort unless revenue is a part of the equation.

The Cyber Pandemic and the Biological Pandemic will always cross the boundaries of Fiction and Non-Fiction because our vulnerability is that we are Human.

Several teaching from every culture state we were made in someone's image. So, every time we as humans try to create, we have a chance to make something in our image. History continues to prove to us from the Garden of Eden, Noah's Ark, Civil Wars, 1914 Christmas Truce, the train to Auschwitz, and our own 21st century that we do not always get it right.

I hope this just triggers thoughts and ideas that reality, be it Real, Virtual, or Augmented, is all around us, and we control the outcome! So, ask questions, remember the future is something we leave for someone else.

Chapter 5

Social Engineering Prevention

Every chapter in life has a beginning and an end. Good times or bad, they eventually pass, but not without leaving a lasting impression on us or teaching us valuable lessons. Similar is the case with the cyber pandemic, it has and will change our lives forever and the lives to come.

We are all influenced by something. We all want to be needed and become a part of something significant. When you think of social engineering, think of someone taking a little part of your soul each time. The greatest social engineering is the art of Marketing. It plays on our weaknesses, our desires, our heartstrings, and our need to leave a legacy. Wanting to dream, desiring something, wanting to be a part of something, and wanting to belong are some normal human emotions that social engineering benefits from. Some items are small that can trick you; some items take time to slowly pull you in. A comment here, a text or chat, or a social site that pulls you in. They are all playing on some emotions, knowing that all humans have weaknesses. Even the bad actors fall for social engineering and get caught.

No corporate training, self-help book, no podcast is going to save you. You are the only one who can think and fend for yourself. History shows that lots of great leaders have major marketing teams to make them immortal and make you idolize their visions. What comes to mind when you think of a person you want to be a part of their click, even if it is only virtual.

We have religious figures that we hope we can stand next to when we walk into the light. We hope to be a part of the six levels of separation from our favorite person. We want to BELONG! That is our weakness; we need to be social, and we need to be a part of the greater view. Even if we do not believe in the end goal, someone is going to provide us with a path. Look at our social media today – we are heavily influenced, from the cars we drive or want to drive, the shoes we have or want, the soap we use to the water we drink, to the fragrance we wear or want to wear.

So, what is it worth to you? A small piece of your soul. If I want you, your loved ones, your data, your life, your vote, the keys to your company's technology or data, I will get it. It may take a few seconds, a few months, or even years, but I will get it. The cyber pandemic is not a thing; it is not a tool; it is not a cause. It is a state of mind, a state of mind that is older than time itself – I want what you have, or what you can do to move me forward, and if you look in the rear-view mirror, you will see all of the loss caused by this driver. Governments and corporations are spending billions of dollars to protect, control, and influence what? COMMERCE!!

The next pages talk about what it is, how it works and why. Again, only you can take control to change the narrative – Ask Why? Think outside the box and remember the most vulnerable are the easiest to destroy.

What Is Social Engineering?

Cyber security is a word that is directly associated with technological vulnerability and the defense mechanisms used against hackers to safeguard data networks. However, it is not just the technological weakness that makes data networks vulnerable; human weakness also factors in the ways organizations and networks can be jeopardized. Taking undue advantage of human weakness coins the term social engineering: the act of extracting sensitive information or gaining access to networks through fraudulent activities.

Social engineers manipulate human feelings, such as curiosity or fear, to carry out schemes and draw victims into their traps.

Certain instances of fraudulent activities and schemes involve acting as an employee, such as IT staff, enabling the extraction and right to other employees' usernames and passwords. The alarming aspect of such schemes is how easily people are willing to divulge sensitive information without taking full precautionary measures and ensuring the request is genuine.

To put it simply, social engineering is the use of manipulation and deception, so people fall prey to schemes that enable access to their data.

The process of social engineering happens in steps. First, the attacker does research to gauge information about the victim to learn potential weaknesses and entry points to exploit the existing protocols and attack. Then, the perpetrator attempts to gain the confidence of the victim, so sensitive information is disclosed and access is open for the attacker to make use of it.

Types of Social Engineering Attacks

There are various types of social engineering attacks. So, it's important to understand the definition of social engineering, as well as how it works. Once the basic modus operandi is understood, it's much easier to spot social engineering attacks.

- **Baiting:** The concept of baiting is, as the name suggests, to trap. Baiting can be as simple as putting malware on a USB drive to be used by someone. Any person who makes use of the USB will have a computer system that is compromised with malware. Malware can be as serious as destroying computers by way of power surges, and the USB stick used for the trap does not cost much.
- **Pretexting:** This method ensures the victim is engaged in a way that entraps them to provide confidential information. The way to deceive the victim is by a pretext that catches their attention. For example, someone taking a simple poll online may be led on to divulge bank account details. Or someone could take hold of a company laptop and pretend to be an auditor, gaining access to the internal systems.
- **Phishing:** The most common form of fraud is phishing attacks. This involves a pretentious email or text from an unknown source seeking private information and details. One of the most common forms of phishing attacks is an email from a bank to verify security details and then redirect them to a fake website that captures the login details. Another instance is 'spear-phishing' wherein a specific

employee from a company is targeted to divulge information from emails supposedly sent from higher-level executives within the organization.

- **Vishing and Smishing:** Both these attacks are different forms of phishing. Voice phishing, or vishing, involves calling a random person and extracting data by queries, and directly asking for information. Smishing, also stylized as SMiShing, on the other hand, involves the use of SMS messaging to contrive sensitive information.
- **Quid pro Quo:** This form of attack involves deceiving people into believing they will get something in exchange for the data they divulge. One such example is scareware, wherein computer users are made to panic and believe that their computer needs an update, but in reality, the update is a threat posed to the system.
- **Contact Spamming and Email Hacking:** This type of attack involves hacking into an individual's email or social media accounts. This kind of access allows correspondence with the victim's contacts and builds the image of dire situations wherein these contacts are asked to wire or transfer money. In other scenarios,

certain links or videos can be shared with the contacts which contain malware or Trojan.

- **Farming vs. Hunting:** The previously mentioned attacks are simple ways of 'hunting' for information and extraction of data. However, there are more advanced forms of attacks. Such attacks have foundations in forming personal and emotional relationships with victims over extended periods for trust-building. Attacks of this nature are known to be 'farming attacks' and are much more serious for the victim and rewarding for the attacker if the infiltration scheme is successful. However, such an attack also holds a greater risk. But, as the saying goes, the greater the risk, the greater the reward.

How to Avoid Social-engineering Attacks?

Social-engineering attacks are way more difficult to fight, given the characteristics of such attacks. The attacks prey on various human aspects such as naivety, curiosity, and personal desires. Therefore, be wary whenever you feel alarmed by an email or an offer displayed on a website that attracts you or when you come across stray digital media lying about. Being alert can help you protect yourself against most social-engineering attacks taking place in the digital realm. Moreover, the following tips can help improve your vigilance in relation to social engineering hacks…

- **Source Check:** Not trusting blindly is one of the easiest ways to avoid attacks. Taking some time to check the source saves people from the many implications of such attacks. Be it a random USB, an email from a bank, or a random phone call saying someone's won a lottery, if it seems suspicious, it must be treated with utmost caution. Checking for the website URL, the email source, and spelling mistakes are small steps to ensuring that the source is authentic. When in doubt, just contacting the official customer service representatives saves all the headache.
- **How Much Do They Know?** It is always advisable to check how much information the source of inquiry is expected to have. For example, if a bank calls, they must possess all the security data prior. If not, the suspicion must be dealt with accordingly.
- **Break the Chain:** Attacks of social engineering depend on creating an urgent situation needing a prompt response so the victims don't think too much. However, giving it a moment to think can be a huge

step toward precaution and prevention. Calling customer service representatives or visiting official websites rather than handing out sensitive information or clicking on random links deters attacks. To crosscheck sources' authenticity, variable forms of communication, such as contacting official representatives, can be adopted.

- **Request ID:** Asking for identification is always a reasonable approach to prevent these attacks. For example, if someone is carrying a box and needs to enter a building, one may first ask for identification and then help the person get in. Similarly, crosschecking personal information such as the name, role, or company of a person calling can be another approach to tackling the issue of social-engineering attacks. In the scenario that a person is unsure and needs to double-check, having a mentality that requests time to double-check ID is a very safe approach to ensure that the source requesting the information is secure.
- **Spam Filter:** The usage of a good spam filter allows suspicious emails to be marked by way of using different kinds of information that determine the source. A good spam filter will detect files, mails, and

links that have suspicious elements attached, such as IP addresses or sender IDs, or assess what the email consists of to filter it out if suspicious.

- **Is It Even Realistic?** These kinds of attacks probe on urgency and, thus, try to deceive the victims by ensuring they are not being analytical and precautionary. This causes victims to lose sight of reality. Assessment of whether a situation is even realistic can be a preventive measure. For example, if contact is stuck out of the country, would they go out of their way to send text messages? Will a Nigerian prince really gift you 10 million dollars? Use your common sense!
- **Slow and Steady Wins the Race:** Just because a sense of urgency arises, it does not entail not being alert. Taking time and thinking through prevents the attackers' schemes. Pressure is one of the key tactics that malicious actors use to gather information. Under such duress, slowing it down and going steady gives one time to think. In most cases, what happens is that attackers, in fear of the law, stop pursuing their motives.
- **Digital Footprint:** Thinking about digital footprint is very important. Given the nature of how information

is treated online through social media, one must ensure to not overshare personal information, as it helps attackers in their attempts. Give as little information as possible, and answer only what you're being asked.

Device Security

Securing devices is helpful even in the event that a social-engineering attack is a success. This is due to the fact that the damage is limited, and it applies to several devices, be it a smartphone, an office network, or an organizational database.

- The security software on your device or devices needs to be up to date. This aids prevention of malware embedded in certain phishing emails. Make sure automatic updates are engaged, or make it a habit to download the latest signatures first thing each day. Periodically check to make sure that the updates have been applied, and scan your system for possible viruses.
- Consistent and frequent updates of software and firmware are essential in the war against cyber-attacks. One example can be the regular updates on security patches.

- Avoid opening emails and attachments if the source seems unreliable. Confirmation of the sources and not opening emails from unknown senders are a few steps that can be taken for prevention.
- Avoid using easy words or repeating the same password for multiple platforms. Using a combination of numbers and alphabets is recommended. If you think your password has been compromised, change it immediately.
- In this day and age, multifactor authentication is a common tool to prevent a system compromise. This form of authentication prevents attackers from getting user credentials and other information. It may involve voice recognition, use of a security device, fingerprinting, or SMS confirmation codes.
- Keep yourself up-to-date with the latest technology when it comes to cyber security. This will allow you to be aware of various methods to tackle these security risks.
- Be prudent when it comes to offers. If something sounds too good to be true, or if something is too enticing, think over it long and hard.

Social engineering is very dangerous because it takes perfectly normal situations and manipulates them for malicious means. However, by being fully aware of how it works and taking basic precautions, you'll be far less likely to become a victim of social engineering.

Thus, organizations should hold training for people working remotely and on premises about patterns to watch to identify a threat. With the growing demand for cyber security all around the globe due to cyber threats, organizations need to invest their time and money into educating their workforce about social engineering and how to safeguard themselves against a possible attack.

As a result, organizations and individuals would have the upper hand and save the company millions of dollars annually because they would know about an attack beforehand and avoid a possible threat. As the saying goes, "Prevention is better than cure!"

As you finish the book, take a few minutes to ask yourself, *"What can I do to help?"* This book makes you question how the cyber pandemic is changing the way you think, the way you work, and the way you live, just as the biological pandemic is doing. If we ignore either of them, they will not go away, and we will lose people we care for.

As with the biological pandemic, the cyber pandemic is slowing, causing the loss of life. It is still in the shadows; one mishap here, one system failure there, but sometime soon, a major event will occur, and we will all stand around as with 9/11 and ask how something of the sort could happen. All the cyberwar engines will go into mutation to block and track down who did it.

So, setting all politics aside, remember that the leaders around the world, and their advisors, are from the flip phone era; they do not understand how fast technology is changing. So, asking open questions to these leaders is not wrong as your children will be inheriting the world. Again – history continues to repeat itself, but we do not have a technology history to build upon, so when we allow the cyber pandemic history to be written, we are the authors and have no one else to blame.

To add insult to injury, all data you put in the cloud will always be found. No company, tool, or system can erase any or all your data. We can put all the privacy laws and processes into place and can even add massive penalties, but someone, somewhere, has made some backup, some replication tool, some failed batch job, or someone with access made a copy just for fun, so all systems retain some part of your data. So, when they want to classify you or find you, they can. But most of us are not worth the effort unless revenue is a part of the equation.

The cyber pandemic and the biological pandemic will

always cross the boundaries of fiction and non-fiction because our vulnerability is that we are human.

Several teaching from every culture state we were made in Someone's image. So, every time we, as humans, try to create, we have a chance to make something in our image. History continues to prove to us from the Garden of Eden, Noah's Ark, Civil Wars, 1914 Christmas Truce, the train to Auschwitz, and our own 21st century that we do not always get it right.

I hope this triggers thoughts and ideas that reality, be it real, virtual, or augmented, is all around us, and we control the outcome! So, ask questions, remember the future is something we leave for someone else.

If this is the real world and you are not under your control, the Metaverse will end up controlling you – every thought, action, the result will be influenced, your alternative view will become a reality, and as with all followers, you will spend wealth at the commercial level with nothing tangible in return and at the emotional level as you try to keep up. A bad actor could also add a pandemic to the metaverse – so you can't hide. The pandemics, biological or cyber, have no level of discrimination.

Someone once said something like- remember if the devil was not real, man would create *he/him/his* - *she/her/hers* -

they/them/they're in our image – Did we?

Chapter 6

Think like an Attacker

"On or about 03:00 UTC, (06:00 Moscow time, UTC+3) on 24 February, Russian President Vladimir Putin announced in a prerecorded television broadcast that he had ordered 'a special military operation' in Eastern Ukraine. Minutes later, missile strikes occurred at dozens of cities across the country,[3] *including Ukraine's capital, Kyiv."*

All the previous data points in this book are coming true, not specific to the attack on the souverain country of Ukraine; this is horrific and continues to prove that humans let to their own devices will destroy the world. The cyber-WW 'D' that has ensued will have a lasting impact well after the world has reset Russia. All headlines are about the price of oil, the price of food, the price of system-processing chips, who is responsible for driving this conflict, and who is standing on the sidelines to profit.

The real impact is unseen to most of the 8+ billion people

around the world; the cyberwar continues to run under the comprehension of the average person. The cost of the destruction, extortion through ransom, and X-ware attacks will not be seen but will be felt directly or indirectly.

When you think of the nation, individual states, or the person in their mother's basement, managing an attack for some reason, think of the anonymous – the masked mercenaries that have entered the WAR, bringing non-conventional weapons to the front lines. They are currently focused on the demon of the day but can also change their focus to any target they want. In parallel are the copycats that want to be a part of the cool cyber elite underground.

Remember, knock-offs from anywhere are knock-offs, and worse are the ones with lesser quality. Bad is bad, but poor-quality bad is even worse; hit and run and no one cares. We have all heard of cyber-attacks, but we sit back and think that protective software, hardware, and antivirus tools that are deployed will protect us so we can keep surfing the web, watching YouTube, and paying our bills with the click of an app. Well, think again!

Just like the COVID-19 biological pandemic, the cyber pandemic is testing all its tricks; the bad actors also have the DNA CRISPR tools – not the same, but we can splice and code any command line, any DLL, and any subroutine to cause an effect. So, taking data hygiene seriously is critical.

As the new cyber tools propagate and are battle-tested, the next target will not need to combat this new cyber variant. Now think of your government, the news, and the social media you believe in and follow like blind rats. All are working to manage your views, your thoughts, and your actions. The tools will be better, the virus, malware, phishing, ransomware, and X-ware will all be stronger, the targets will be more precise, and the impact will be greater.

Every data center and server room that controls the things you take for granted are under attack; the good guys with the shields are keeping this at bay, but just wait. The simple Borg Command 'SLEEP' can be leveraged for every technology stack in the world. The fan in your computer is told to stop, and the thermal sensor is told not to react. Voila, you have a meltdown. Think of this on a massive scale – all of Russia's technology stacks start to fail – networks, banks, insurance companies, trading floors, power, cooling, water treatment, hence everything. Then, the ethics fall to the wayside – hospitals, children's nurseries, treatment centers, and every other system you leverage. Whoopee – we got the bad guys!!

No, you enabled the same forces that you think you

control or influence and extort you. Just like a rogue nuclear state, you have a standoff of the ultimate destruction. The issues will be just like the biological pandemic – it will be slow and painful, and you will see it playing out from global region to global region. The general concern will rise to greater demands and civil unrest to heavy-handed responses as each of you will be challenging the governments on why they can not stop this. Services will stop, the haves and have nots will have a greater wedge driven between them, and we will look like a page out of the book Soylent Green.

How will you work to slow this? Not unlike app, pandemics starts the need to rise to help prevent the unknown outcome. One way is to step back and look at the facts – some will be fuzzy, some will be colored, and some will be downright lies. But as your mother always said, there is some truth in every lie.

Now let's talk facts. You are not smart enough to understand how this will all play out. As the world gets smaller and we encroach on places and things we should not, how would we know that eating a bat would cause a pandemic? How would we know the theory of HIV jumping from a green monkey to humans would cause an AIDS pandemic? It can all be conjecture, but the results are the same – people die!

So, with technology, virus and cyber pandemics will have the same outcome. Going to places you do not understand and ingesting data into your systems that you do not understand will have the same results – people will die. People in power, people that want power, and nations that want control or influence will all embrace the unknown, as making a pact with the devil can be easier than making a pact with someone or something that you trust. With trust comes commitment.

With the devil, it is just your soul, and, today, it is not critical you will deal with that later. Trust is hard work, and you need to continue to reinsure it is working. Just like updating your antivirus, changing your password, thinking before you click, and not propping open the door take time, and understanding if I do not care, someone else will. That other person will only be able to push that rock up a hill for you so long before they walk away and trust is broken. Then the cyber pandemic starts all over, and the next generation picks up the dead and tries to restart.

As was stated in the previous chapters, we have a new enemy that has no conscience, and the impact will be, and is, dire. You laugh, the terminator will never happen. If it does, it might be cool as a tool against my foes.

It is real; every company in the world is pushing Machine Learning (ML) and Artificial Intelligence (AI) to help manipulate data and, indirectly and directly, YOU. So, as these algorithms get better and they learn and make the decision, are you getting the best price for, say, insurance? So, how did they get that data? Today, you provided it; tomorrow, your car, plane, or computer will. So what are the consequences?

Someone said during the Russian-Ukraine war that posting something to a social site could get a Russian person or their aging parents arrested and their lives destroyed. So, exposing your parents to a biological event could cause the same outcome. Every click you make is tracked, all this data is collected in some database, and every database can or has been hacked, so someone or something knows who you are, what you think, and how to use that against you.

Blackmail is blackmail, no matter how you think about it. It can be in the form of shaming, influencing your decisions, political lemmingism (new word), and all of this has been accomplished by data that you have given someone access to through wanting to belong, wanting to be cool, general naivety, or plain stupidity. Every survey you respond to, every app you click on, and every URL you accept captures the data needed to influence you, identify you, and profile you.

People of all colors can feel profiled, but this is a new reality. The cyber-world does not care what color you are, who you sleep with, or how you identify yourself. But it does profile you and will target you with opportunities and, in the future (that is now), will use this against you.

GDPR and the other 49 versions being mapped or in place around the world try to add a level of protection, but, really, they think that someone or some tool will remove all your habits from a database housed on the Dark Web or in a government-agency vault. The question is, who is watching the hen house. Knowledge is power, and knowing who, what, and when is the oldest lever that can be pulled.

We have talked about AI, ML, governments, bad actors, and your need to belong and be a part of something as your real life, in general, is meaningless. Now we are in WW 'D', and what you have given up will be used against you. But what about the future generations? The ones that have no idea about what they have given up, the schools have no clue, the religious organizations have no clue, and believe it or not, the governments have not a clue. Be it biological or cyber; we are moving so fast that the only ones that will win are the ones that can think in 3D.

THINKING IN 3D? The ability to think outside of the box, the people that brought you the moon, Mars, and the Rubik's cube. 99.99999% of the globe thinks in 1D. Maybe 2D, but only a few can think in 3D. Now you are moving into the alternative reality (AR, Virtual Reality (VR), or Inception Reality (IR)). Your need to belong is so strong that you are exiting current 1D into 3D, let's say, someone's metaverse. You can be anyone you want, play in any space you want, or buy anything you want if you have enough cryptocurrency and hide.

I am calling BS on this model; you are hiding in plain sight. Every digital process you use, I can track, and your governments can track. No, it is all encrypted, and the cloud is safe. If you believe that I have some land in virtual Florida, I will sell you. The cyber pandemic, like the biological pandemic, has infiltrated your metaverse; it has not shown its avatar face, but it is watching you, it is watching your children, and it is influencing you, and you do not even know it.

3D has its advantages – we can look for new solutions; we can build new algorithms to address 1D problems. But they all come at a price – your data, your thoughts, your actions. Remember, out of war, we have all types of innovations that change the world. The cyberwar being waged today will influence tomorrow. Your tomorrow will be in 3D, so when we declare war within the metaverse, do you think taking off your headset will reset this?

No, AI, ML, and IR will keep playing, and they will figure out how to span the technology void between 1D and 3D, and this will happen because you cannot think in 3D. Why do you think we have a chip shortage? Yes, we have lots of elements needed to create a processor, but the element that is driving this direction is you. You need every experience to be faster, more real, and 1D-like. The technology you drive is the reason for us going to war and taking control of the elements needed. Not me, really? Look at the elements. Who is mining them? Who is building them? They are your cyber slaves. I would not buy a product that a small child builds, mines, or dies for. All this data is driving your decisions, pinging you when you are near that mall, that store, or that drive-thru.

So, if I am collecting all of that data, and you do not care to protect it, then why am I the bad guy that compromises it, sells it, extorts it, and can change your life, your company's life? It is not my fault; I pay other people to protect me. Your mother did not teach you to look both ways crossing a street. It is her fault that you get hit by a truck walking into traffic because you can't take your eyes off the event on your phone and that the data you gave up is being used to keep you focused on something that is not relevant. It seems like a real copout to blame your mother. Everyone in this world is responsible.

Now, your entire world could come crashing down; the global internet is under siege. Over one million cyber-attacks were reported within an hour. The edge and the internet, cable, and mobile providers are using every tool they must to keep it looking like all is smooth. They are not providing you with the real story. If they go offline, capitalism will go offline. Many governments already run outside of the internet to limit the exposure and maintain critical processes and communications operational, but this leaves you in the dark.

Just like the start of the biological pandemic, only a few had any idea what humanity would be up against. Even now, only a few can understand what we are up against. Government requests for corporations to harden security is not for your protection but for the top companies to keep the economies running and tax revenue flowing. Have you seen a request to the masses asking for help?

You need to take this on yourself; you need to be your family's cyber mercenary. You will not be writing code or developing the next firewall and AV tools (maybe) but following the basic processes and explaining to your family what the risks are. You lose everything – lots of commercials point to having your identity stolen, your home titles stolen, or worse. These ads have a lot of fear and bending of light, but they are based on reality. I cannot stress enough to follow basic guidelines. Your parents, your children, and you are vulnerable, and no one is going to bail you out.

Chapter 7

2022 and Cyber Security

Mommy! My phone has a virus! YUCK!

The easiest way to introduce ransomware into your environment is through your children. Managing the apps your children download not only allows you to manage what they are seeing or who is seeing them but also check if they are secure. Apple and Google try to scan them, but the bad actors are getting good. The initial app is clean, but the URL to updates and links may not be. The cyber pandemic can hit homes faster than you can open the app. Your phone tracks every one of their moves – where they are, when they get off the bus. Do you know who they think their friends are? When they talk about child trafficking, it is not only in a far-off country; it is at home. They can pick up your kid, and a life of sex trade and abuse is all they will know, and you will never see them again. If you do, they are broken like a shell that will never trust anyone.

According to research by GuardChild, only 1/3 of households with Internet access protect their children with filtering or blocking software. So, if you think it is just an app and someone else's tools will protect your data and your family, you are wrong. If your child tried to eat gum they found on the underside of a table, you would take them to urgent care, but if they are making friends with online people you do not know, do you care? I guess not!

Horrific Child Abduction Statistics and Facts

Around 8 million children are reported missing each year worldwide.

An estimated 2,300 children are reported missing daily in the US.

Teenagers are the most common age group for abduction.

Less than 1% of missing children get taken by strangers.

More than 90% of abductions are a deed of one of the parents.

A child is reported missing every two minutes in Europe.

77% of victims of online predators are aged 14 or older.

69% of teens regularly receive requests for communication from strangers online and don't inform a parent.

If you do care, then you better step back and talk about

the subject, know what they have on their phone, and explain what could happen. Your children, at any age, can pull up porn, so you might want to discuss it. Some kids in school might be showing it off as their parents do not think it is a big deal. Just think!

Your family is fully exposed; your router is open, and so someone in the world is watching you. The cyber pandemic has released a whole new set of peeping toms: cyber-watchers. They are leveraging every access point you have. Now they can control your life, your business, your decisions, and, yes, they resell the images of you, your children, and access to your home to the highest bidder.

Now the safety nets are gone; you are all alone in the cyber pandemic. You have not heeded any recommendations and think you are immune. So, you can skip the antivirus, the mask, and the best practices, and you have no one to blame. You do not have cyber protection insurance; you do not have a backup; you do not know what to do. So, think before you say it will not happen to me. It already has!

Today, another set of events occurred. Not only is the cyber pandemic at a high point, but the direct attacks are also looking to cause a direct impact on human life. Every email or app you hit has the potential of initiating a major event, and each one will continue to pale against the last.

Many are not even reported, as the teams that could track them are overwhelmed. There is not a centralized process like CDC or WHO. If there was, they would not be looking out for you, the masses. Today, we are targeting greater and greater infrastructure, looking to blackout our foes. As the military expenditure on weapons increased to levels not seen in our lifetime, the cyber forces are funded with a small percentage of the leftovers.

The flip-phone generation is doing what everyone is doing – what they know. They know how to blow things up, but the cyber defenses and offenses know that the bad actors have the upper hand. As you think of explosions and the horrors they can and do cause, the cyber horrors will be even worse.

The cyber exposure will slowly take over the world as you know it; you will see lives destroyed from the inside, the stress, no support, no understanding, and no help from leadership. The only ones that will help are the ones in it for a profit.

This could start with a small drop in your credit score—a small charge on a credit card or bank account. Maybe a few extra apps charges to your account. They are small, so you will look at them later. It has caught up with you – your score is destroyed, and your employer has alerts and starts to question your capability – can they trust you? Do they want to trust you? Are you worth them standing up with you, or are you too much of a liability to their brand?

I do not need to tell you how this will play out. On the job, with no credit score, no income, and no support, it will spiral out of control. Your spouse cannot take the stress; the kids feel you have scared them, and all the physical things everyone needs are gone. Can you rebuild and redefine what you are and who you are? It is not easy, but you have options.

First, you need to define who you and your family are. Take a yearly snapshot of what bills you have, what mortgage you have, what car and loans you have. Your kids' expense reports, your annual review at work. Photos of events that only you or your family were a part of. Put this in an envelope, have a cover letter notarized, and mail it to yourself (have the postal clerk stamp the back of the envelope). Do not open it when you receive it. Put them each year in a safety deposit box. If an event happens, then you have governmental proof, a timestamp, that the courts need to accept. If someone takes your identity, it will happen, and you can go to court, but you will have validated proof of who you are.

A backup process is also to have tracking turned on – this is a little scary, but if you need to prove that you were not at a place and time, this can provide secondary data. But it also can be leveraged by your government – all of the big companies – all of your data is for sale legitimately, even if it is kind of protected by GDPR or like PI laws. But as we have said before, you are not that important for the government to track you or even help if you encounter a problem.

Chapter 8

Deception

The world is standing on the edge. We have countries playing games while people die. We have leaders playing their last card because they do not care. We have leaders trying to play the intermediary as the outcome is 100% economic – they do not care about the people – we will always make more, and the new generation are followers not leaders. Ask yourself – if you got on a plane to stand on the front lines or logged onto the NET to start a cyber-attack, would your government come get you? Unless *Time Magazine* flagged it, we would say not. All we can say is good luck, and I hope St. Peter holds the gate open for you.

Unrest is brewing on a global basis – the Americas are set for a civil war; NATO is trying to figure out what to do and the fallout – will all of them be classified as Romania after WWI? Did they side with the wrong team? Who is going to commit Jauhar to protect their people? Today, it is the people caught between the west and the east. The arms race is now a cyber race. We have moved from the pandemic to a cyber arms race. Every country is either trying to be the top dog or catch the top dog.

Technology, Machine Learning, Artificial Intelligence, and all the other versions are converging. The human mind is not able to grasp what the outcome will be, but the target today is data. The one that controls, influences, or modifies the data wins. Today, you are looking for insight on WWIII; you can select news sites from every country, from national to local, and they all have a twist.

People die because of cyber wars, even if no bullets are ever fired. Instead, they die in emergency rooms that no longer have power, from broken medical communication networks, and from riots. All of this has happened before. It will happen again. And now, with Russia poised to invade Ukraine and Russian cyberattacks already in motion, we can only hope and pray that what promises to be the first major European war since World War II doesn't spark the next World War.

If it does, I fear the proximate cause won't be Russian T-90 main battle tanks trying to smash their way into Ukraine's capital, Kyiv. It will be the Russian GRU Sandworm hacking group launching a cyberattack that perhaps wrecks the European Union power grid, knocks out major US internet sites such as Google, Facebook, and Microsoft, or stops 4G and 5G cellular services in their tracks. Sound like something out of a modern-day Tom Clancy novel? I wish. This is all too real.[36]

In the past, it was the top US news agency, the AP, that set the baseline. Today, all news is modified to meet the needs of the country, city, company, or politicians' interests. Pick a local China paper, a local Philippine paper, a local Iowa paper, or a South African paper. Then look at the minor differences that influence those readers not only with the story but the information and ads that are associated with the story. You think you have an independent mind and can reason out the facts. You do not know what the facts are. Did someone bomb a hospital physically? Did they bomb it with a cyber-attack? Now read the stories from all points on the globe, and it either be that it was a bomb or it was staged; someone will point out a time stamp on an image, someone will say they were watching it happen, but their IP address will show them thousands of miles away.

But you do not pull this data in; you are trusting a view that you want to hear or read. Only 20% of global readers finish the article or press release. They read the words they want to, and your preprogrammed mind does the rest. We have telephone tags on a global scale.

Malware doesn't care about borders. Past malware such

---

[36] https://www.computerworld.com/article/3647879/will-world-war-iii-begin-in-cyberspace.html

as NotPetya and WannaCry began as nation-state attackware, then quickly went well beyond their original targets. To this day, they're still causing trouble.

The Russian cyberattack on Ukraine has already begun. On Jan. 14, a massive website attack smeared Ukrainian government websites with a warning to "be afraid and expect the worst." That caught headlines, but it was purely a psychological attack.[37]

If I wanted to start a rumor that the great garbage patch in the ocean is fake, it would not take much. A few strategically placed messages on boards, maybe a photo with a government presentation, talking about distraction tactics to keep the general population off the real topic. Even China and North Korea determined that they cannot block all internet or mobile news, but they can influence what their people read, thinking it is from the west. We could and do the same. Just think, if we influenced all children that soda products were being used for mind control by our schools and parents, what do you think the impact on the manufacturer, the supply chain, and the economy would be? So, when you shrug off the cyber pandemic as a biological pandemic, people will believe anything that gives them an easy way out –

---

[37] https://www.computerworld.com/article/3647879/will-world-war-iii-begin-in-cyberspace.html

someone else to blame.

What is the saying? Even if they say something bad about you in the press, it is better than not being talked about at all. Political leaders across the globe are using your lack of questioning to drive your views. AI and ML are being used in the cyberwar to drive your views. Step back and think who really is behind the green Curtin, the great and powerful Oz, or is it just a nerd's self-establishing code generator that is not driving you?

Chapter 9

Post-apocalypse

Well, every event has occurred. The biological pandemic is moving into the shadows; we have forgotten about the loss of life, we have forgotten about the protocols, and the masks blowing across the busy intersections is the last reminder. You have been influenced to be distracted by inflation and high gas prices, and you do not even know why. The biological pandemic left large holes in the supply chain. Social unrest and the drive for inclusion have driven up pay for the general public. Still, all of that has driven up the overall cost, and the global mass' exit from the workforce is adding to the cracks.

The cyber pandemic has impacted every walk of your life, and you do not even realize it. WW3 moves from a war of impact to a war of influence and ongoing insecurity.

Now you need to have a reality check. Have you changed any way you access data, services, or the web? NO! You are still waiting for us to protect you; you cannot take responsibility because you do not want to take responsibility; your children do not want to take responsibility.

The governments lay out policies, laws, and funding, but you cannot fix the problem you do not understand. Generational lack of management provides us the ability to manage, influence, and drive change from afar. White hats and black hats continue to battle it out across the DMZ, but you forget about the few of us that are influencers. We do not care about you; we do not care about the outcome. We care about how we control the outcome. We will tell you that you do not need a mask, or we will tell you that you need a mask. We will provide you an Antivirus software that provides some protection, but like a vaccine, you will need to keep getting updates that will cost you the overall system, but we will get rich. You will follow us and provide us with all of the data, habits, and geolocation data we want in exchange for a false sense of security. Like all pandemics, the events are all for good at the start, but as time goes on, the economic.com benefits outweigh the dotherightthing.org benefits.

The cyber pandemic will never end if you do not take some control and think before you click!

101 back to the basics; maybe a few leaders, teachers, and parents are thinking about the future – how much time the next generation is spending online being influenced, but people and processes they themselves cannot contemplate. Starting with the basics can help rebuild the emotional and technological wasteland that we call home.

You are running from safe zone to safe zone. You are trying to keep yourself and your close ones from being impacted by biological death, cyber-induced deaths, or the slow erosion of the world as you know it. In five years, cyber-attacks and stolen identities will be as common as trash on every street corner. In ten years, you will not be leaving your homes; the social unrest will be managed through walled and guarded neighborhoods, both physical and cyber protected.

The 2022 cyber pandemic is now listed as a cyberwar by the US Government. This will impact your lives. PowerGrid's, water system, satellite, communications, this will not be lights out, but a slow degradation of services, higher costs, and, yes, you, and those with you, will assist in this downward spiral. Every time you take a chance and access sites, apps, and networks without thinking about the risks, you provide the bad actors from around the world and even in your backyard the keys to access controls.

What, I do not have access to any of that stuff? Maybe not, but you have access to systems and apps and are letting the bad actors get to your passwords and your companies' VPN. Bypassing standard security processes at home, school, or work allows the bad actors to find a path to the larger prize.

IT may take years to map a route, but when they are

tracked back, it is you that opened the first door. This is like leaving your child or pet in a hot car. It will only be for a minute when I grab something. Time runs on, and guess what, someone died! This is extreme, but when you let someone access something, the end goal will be the same. Can you sleep knowing that you may have allowed the power to a hospital to go offline?

"Don't click there. Don't do that." Employees know the drill. Cybersecurity teams hope these warnings will keep employees from doing something that will put the organization at risk, and rightfully so. Research conducted in 2016 showed that 91% of cyber-attacks started with phishing emails. The number of insider threat incidents has also increased by 47% over the last two years. Whether there is malicious intent or not, statistics like these are why security teams view their employees as a gateway for hackers to infiltrate the network.

In 2020, enterprises underwent enormous change. Many employees now work from homes spread out around the globe. The pandemic has created a fundamental shift in how workers connect to their company networks, use their company-issued devices, and complete their tasks.

With all of these additional distractions, ensuring your teams are cyber aware is more critical than ever before. Will they be as diligent and cautious in the comfort of their own home?

Will the vast increase in access points give attackers another advantage in this never-ending chess match?[38]

Fifteen years from now, it will not be the Terminator, but we will continue to be more dependent on robotics, Machine Learning, and Artificial Intelligence. Today, a number of critical brain and specialty surgeries are performed by robotic processes. So, as we move more into this area of robots performing critical or mundane roles, the exposure, risk, and outcome are in our hands. If they screw up, it is because the code was incorrect, the algorithms were incorrect, and the quality and review were not followed. This could be driven by getting the most revenue and letting the lawyers work out the impact; a bad actor got access to a low-level command that was not seen as a risk but was able to build a bridge. Every action has a reaction.

Back to what you instill in your children, the next generation could be from the basic question. What are the ten things he, she, or other classification is learning in school and at home? Ask the teachers if they have the tools and training to help bridge this technology void. Offer up someone from your company security team to provide basic training. Look for a YouTube video that will get them interested – they can be enticed

---

[38] https://www.securitymagazine.com/articles/94027-the-first-line-of-defense-why-employees-are-the-key-to-stronger-cybersecurity

by Teletubbies, Barney, and Game of Thrones; they can pick up the basics. Make them the superhero, so as they grow, they know that the cyber pandemic/WW3 is real.

Back to 2022, step back and look at what you are doing every day. You do not have time to do this! If you do not, no one else will. Again, the flip-phone generation running the world has no clue. The cyber divisions are the younger generations trying to help the flip-phone generation understand reality. Make sure your child is a part of this movement instead of standing on the sidelines like you are.

Milk, bread, fuel, medications, and Internet costs will increase by 40% this year. You will pay them, and the costs will become the new norm. That has nothing to do with a cyber pandemic/war! The material war is just the front; the cyberwar is now the fabric of society on a global basis. Just like the biological pandemic, 99.999999% of the population still does not understand who, what, and how these things happen. It cannot get any simpler – a Zika Miskito gets on a plane, travels to point x, is pregnant, and from generation to generation, they now have a foothold and cannot be eradicated.

This is the same with a biological or cyber virus. You may be able to manage the event, but you will never be able to eliminate it. Why? Just like TB and polio, we had it eradicated, but someone felt they did not need to get the vaccination for what the reason, and now it is back. The cyber process works the same. One open port will give the underbelly of the internet the access they need to redeploy a virus variant we thought we had controlled.

Chapter 10

Someone once said something like – 'Remember, if the devil was not real, man would create *he/him/his, she/her/hers, they/them/their* in their image.' Did we do that?

You're thinking this book repeats itself a lot; it does. As they say, you need to say something seven times for people to remember it. The cyber pandemic or cyberwar is not going away; you are a part of its fabric. You cannot fix everything, but every war has had a saying to help people think.

The devil, no matter who he or she is, is using the tools we provide them to bring confusion and evil into your life. Before you blame someone or something, ask who will benefit from the outcome. It will not be you! But you are giving the demons of the cyber world the access.

2022

Think before you click.

Everything you do is being tracked.

Technology Trust - can you prove it is real?

1942

If everyonc is thinking alike, someone isn't thinking.

Loose lips sink ships.

They are always listing.

Your name is unknown. Your deed is immortal.

Don't let that shadow touch them!

The rest of the pages are blank. It is time for you to draft your own story that will either help with base understanding or play ignorant and let everyone else take the blame. I have been told there are no atheists in a foxhole. When something bad happens, asking your God *'why'* is not going to turn back time. You have been enabled with the power of reason and decision-making. If you play the part of a lemming, then being on the wrong side of the cliff is your doing and no one else's.

Chapter 1. (I was born…)

____

____

____

____

____

____

____

You make your last entry as the earth stands still, holding what is dear – a photo, your child, your doll – and all because you opened the door, just a crack.

Signed,

Humanity

Made in the USA
Monee, IL
21 August 2022

59050444-f5a3-42ba-bea5-5f896664a3eeR01